THE COURTS AND FREEMASONRY

THE COURTS AND FREEMASONRY

Case histories that have or could affect Freemasonry

By

ALPHONSE CERZA,

A Special Edition of
Research Lodge No. 2 A.F. & A.M. of Iowa

Jerry Marsengill, Editor

Published by
Anchor Communications
Highland Springs, Virginia

Distributed by: Macoy Publishing and Masonic Supply Co., Inc., Richmond, VA 23228

Copyright © 1986 by Research Lodge No. 2, AF & AM, Iowa

All rights reserved. No part of this book may be reproduced by any means whatsoever without written permission from the publisher. Address inquiries to: Anchor Communications, Drawer 70, Highland Springs, VA 23075-0070

Printed in the United States of America

ISBN No. 0-935633-03-0

SPECIAL APPRECIATION TO

Alphonse Cerza for this unselfish gift to Freemasonry in making his manuscript on court cases involving fraternal organizations which have affected Freemasonry, but especially for his untiring efforts to lenhance the literature of the Craft, thereby adding to the knowledge of its members along with that of the general public.

Research Lodge No. 2, A.F. & A.M., Iowa

FOREWORD

The person who said "there is nothing new under the sun" spoke a truism that is still prevalent. As will be noted from the pages of this book, the attacks against Freemasonry are not new. They have been going on for centuries.

And there's nothing new about these attacks. The same old arguments are being repeated over and over again. Today the answers to these critics are the same as they have been for centuries. It's interesting to note that the courts, in almost every case, have provided the answers to these bigots.

"Freemasonry is a religion" is a claim heard over and over again. The courts have ruled on many occasions that this claim is false. "It is a secret organization" is another cry of the critics. As far back as 1861 the courts said this is also false. As one court noted: "The purpose and objects of the society have been made public in numerous books, periodicals, and public addresses." Since 1861 thousands more books, periodicals, and other tracts have been added to the public statements of the Craft.

Alphonse Cerza, a noted attorney, professor of law, and respected Freemason, has once again provided the honored society of Freemasons with a valuable publication. He has made a life-long study of law and the principles of Freemasonry. Each of his publications is now a classic. Each has provided the Craft with knowledge it could receive nowhere else.

Anti-Masonry has been with us since before the formation of the Grand Lodge system that began in 1717. Cerza has studied this subject in greater detail than anyone else. What he has learned he has made available to anyone interested in learning the truth about Freemasonry.

"A very substantial part of the activity of this order is devoted to the help of those who are needy and in distress," said a court in 1910. Today over two million dollars a day is spent by Freemasonry to help those in need; most of it goes to men, women, and children who have no connection with Masonry. One might ask the critics: "How much does *your* organization spend to help others in distress who are not believers of your doctrine?" A truthful answer would probably be: "Little, or nothing."

Within the pages of this book are found the answers to those who belittle Freemasonry. Most important, these answers are provided by learned judges—not Freemasons.

Without question, this book should be in the library of every Lodge, Grand Lodge, interested Freemason, and critic of the Craft.

Alphonse Cerza has done an outstanding job in the areas of law and Freemasonry. In 1931 he received the Juris Doctor degree from Loyola University and since then has practiced, written about and taught the subject. He became a Master Mason in Waubansia Lodge No. 160, now Decalogue No. 160, in Illinois. His writings for the Craft have been numerous.

Cerza belongs to several Research Lodges and is a Life Fellow and Past President of The Philalethes Society. In 1986 he received one of the first Distinguished Service Medals of the Society for his work for Freemasonry in general. He has been cited several times by the Scottish Rite. He is one of the few Americans who has been made a full member of Quatuor Coronati Lodge No. 2076, London, England. He is a Blue Friar, an organization of Masonic authors, and an original member of The Masonic Brotherhood of the Blue Forget-Me-Not, which honors Masonic educators. He holds the Frederic Dalcho Award, the Medal of Excellence of the Masonic Lodge of Research of Connecticut, the Virginia Craftsmen Distinguished Service Medal, and others.

Any publication from the pen of Alphonse Cerza can be relied on for accuracy. We are proud to present another of his publications, another of his gifts to the Craft he loves. It is a work of reference that will grow even more valuable with time.

Allen E. Roberts

PREFACE

The court is the agency utilized in civilized communities to settle disputes which arise between persons relating to the law. Freemasonry consists of members as well as the organization and since they do not exist in a vacuum or function in a glass enclosed tower there have been occasions when disputes have arisen within the Craft. The courts are then required to determine the conflict. In countries outside the United States the Craft has rarely had occasion to go to court to settle disputes. In the United States, however, there have been about four hundred court cases which have resulted in appeals and have ended with the issuance of a formal written opinion by the court. These opinions appear in the official printed volumes of the specific court and can be read in the law libraries of many court houses, bar associations, and public libraries.

These opinions are of importance to us because they illustrate how Masonic problems have been determined by the courts and they indicate how the Craft in its functioning, at times, must adjust itself to comply with these decisions. These opinions of the court make interesting reading because of their factual content as well as to the rules that are selected by the courts in arriving at their decisions. There is no assurance, of course, that decisions made in such cases will be followed in the future. Laws change and the facts in each case are not always the same.

Only a limited number of these cases can be discussed on a practical basis, so a selection has been made of interesting situations, the general law principles involved, and the possibility that similar situations may arise again, and therefore, some guidance is needed. In some instances pertinent language used by the court in its opinion will be reproduced. This is done because the rules of law are set out authoritatively, and to illustrate how judges rationalize and arrive at their decisions with the use of general rules which are applied to specific problems.

This is not intended to be a complete or detailed presentation of every reported court case which directly or indirectly covers the Craft and other fraternal organizations. This should be recognized because if you have a problem which is not covered here it will be necessary to do some research to see if such a situation has been covered in a reported case. There are enough cases presented here to illustrate the problems which have existed and how general rules of law have been applied by the appellate tribunals.

Citation of authorities are given in order to assist those readers who may wish to pursue the specific topic in greater detail. Court cases involving other fraternal groups can sometimes be helpful in deciding Masonic questions because the situations may be analogous. The courts themselves do this on occasion. For example: In Re Estate of Lowe, 326 Pa. 375, 192 Atl. 405 (1937), the court was considering the validity of a gift made in a will to the Odd Fellows Home and in its opinion the court considered the case of Philadelphia v. Masonic Home of Pennsylvania, 160 Pa. 572, 28 Atl. 954 (1894). Anyone making a study of problems concerning the Craft may at times be required to consult cases involving other fraternal groups, such as, the Elks, Moose, Knights of Pythias, and so on.

Many of the cases mentioned here do not involve Masonic organizations. They are covered because they illustrate the application of general legal principles which may exist in Masonic and other fraternal organizations. Cases involving insurance benefit associations which restrict their membership to Masons (many of which existed years ago) are not covered.

It must be borne in mind when reading these cases that there is a large body of Masonic law that is separate from the general rules of law applicable to everyone in the community. These rules govern the internal affairs of Freemasonry and are not considered here, but, are covered in Mackey's *Jurisprudence of Freemasonry*; John W. Simons, *Familiar Treatise of the Principle & Practice of Masonic Jurisprudence*; Luke A. Lockwood, *Masonic Law and Practice*, and Henry M. Look, *Masonic Trials*.

Occasionally a court decision will consider these internal rules in arriving at its decision. For example, in Woolfork's Appeal, 126 Pa. St. 47 (1889), (involving a black group calling itself Masonic) it was observed by the court that "The ancient landmarks of the Masonic fraternity are unalterable. On the ancient landmarks are predicated the rules that govern the Masonic fraternity. Nothing can be adopted in derogation of these landmarks." Masonic law was also considered in Smith v. Smith, 2 Desaus 557 (1813; So. Car.) and in Bayliss v. Grand Lodge of Louisiana, 131 La 579, 59 So. 996 (1912).

Anyone desiring to make a further study of this subject should consult such standard law books as *Corpus Juris, Corpus Juris Secuneum* and *American Jurisprudence*. The topics to consult are "Associations", "Benefit Societies" and "Fraternal Groups." In reading this material it is important to note that in recent years the courts have begun to make a distinction between "social" organizations (such as Freemasonry) and groups such as trade unions, professional associations, trading exchanges, etc. which affect a member's right to earn a living. (6 Am. Juris. 2d 461).

If you are presented with a specific legal problem, before arriving at a definite answer, a lawyer should be consulted. Get the benefit of his experience and learn if there have been any recent changes in the law on the subject in which you are interested.

HOW TO USE THIS MATERIAL

Here are some guide lines for using the material that is covered within these pages. After each case a citation is given showing where the opinion can be found. An explanation of the citation is as follows: the first number is the volume of the official book where the opinion in the case is printed; the abbreviation is the name of the state Supreme Court rendering the opinion; if the citation has "App." after the name of the state, the opinion was rendered by the Appellate Court of the State. The next number is the page. The year stated is the time the opinion was rendered. If additional information is shown this may relate to another place where the opinion is reproduced.

For example, Robinson v. Yates City Lodge, 86 Ill. 589 (1877), is explained as follows—The "86" refers to volume 86 of the official reports; the "Ill." refers to the State of Illinois where the case was decided; the "598" refers to the page in the volume where the decision appears. The "(1887)" refers to the year the decision was rendered. When additional information appears it refers to other places where the opinion of the court is reproduced.

Another example, "21 N. E. 635" would indicate that the opinion is reproduced in volume 21 North Eastern Reporter on page 635. These volumes are privately published and are widely used.

ABBREVIATIONS

All E. R.—All English Reports (Cases decided in England)
Am. Juris. 2d.—*American Jurisprudence,* second edition (a legal encyclopedia)
Eng. & Am. Ency.—*English and American Encyclopedia of Law* (an old Encyclopedia of law)
Atl.—*Atlantic Reporter* (Privately printed collection of cases)
C. J.—*Corpus Juris* (A legal encyclopedia)
C. J. S.—*Corpus Juris Secondum* (A legal encyclopedia bringing up to date the material in Corpus Juris)

N. E.—*Northeastern Reporter* (Private collection of cases)
Pac.—*Pacific Reporter* (Private collection of cases)
So.—*Southern Reporter* (Private collection of cases)
S. W.—*Southwestern Reporter* (Private collection of cases)
A. L. R.—*American Law Reports* (Private collection of selected cases with annotations of additional cases on the subject)

Although this book will not be read as one would a novel, I believe it will prove interesting reading. Perhaps its greatest value will be as a reference volume. It has been my experience that the law is an extremely interesting topic. It is something most of us will come in contact with at least once during our lifetime.

If this helps just one person, my reward will be great. Read it. Study it. Most of all, enjoy it.

Alphonse Cerza
Riverside, Illinois
   July 4, 1986

CONTENTS

Foreword vii
Preface ix

I. THE NATURE OF FREEMASONRY 1

II. THE MASONIC ORGANIZATION
   2.1 Legal Existence of Organization................. 9
   2.2 Majority of Members Cannot Dissolve Group 10
   2.3 Organization Can Only Act Within
       Powers Granted 12
   2.4 Right to Exclusive Use of Name................ 13
   2.5 Irregular Groups 17
   2.6 Liability of Non-Member Using
       Emblem of Group 18
   2.7 Grand Lodge Rights and Powers................ 19
   2.8 Business Activities of Organization............. 21
   2.9 Property Right Cases 23
   2.10 Provisions in Wills............................ 25
   2.11 Power to Exclude Membership in Other Groups.. 29
   2.12 Liability for Injuries........................... 31
   2.13 No Personal Liability for Opposing
       Membership or Charter 32

III. MASONIC MEMBERSHIP CASES
   3.1 Admission of Member is a Privilege 35
   3.2 Constitutional Right to Select Associates......... 35
   3.3 Jurisdiction 40
   3.4 Termination of Membership 42
   3.5 Procedure in Termination Cases................. 45
   3.6 Courts Have Limited Powers in
       Termination Cases 45
   3.7 Right of Members to Property of Group 48

IV. TAXATION AND FREEMASONRY
   4.1 Real Estate Tax Cases 51
   4.2 Inheritance Tax Cases 62
   4.3 Estate Tax Cases.............................. 63
   4.4 Miscellaneous Tax Cases 64

V. COURT TRIALS
    5.1 Parties to Suit 65
    5.2 Must Exhaust Remedies With
         Organization Before Suit 66
    5.3 Remedies Available 66
    5.4 Mason as Judge in a Masonic Case.............. 67
    5.5 Mason as Juror in a Masonic Case 69
    5.6 Final Argument Making Reference to the Craft... 70
    5.7 Evidence....................................... 71
    5.8 Libel and Slander Cases 73
    5.9 Confidential Communication Between Masons ... 75
    5.10 Embezzlement Cases 76

VI. MISCELLANEOUS CASES 79
Appendix.. 85
Bibliography 87

I. THE NATURE OF FREEMASONRY

There have been occasions when courts have described the nature of the Craft. Here are some illustrations of what has been said in these court opinions.

In Burdine v. Grand Lodge of Alabama, 37 Ala 478 (1861), the courts said on page 482:

> The purpose and objects of the society have been made public in numerous books, periodicals, and public addresses. From all these sources of information, and from generally received and accredited judgement of the public, the sole purpose and object with which Masonic institutions acquire money and property beyond their current expenses as a society (furniture, light, fuel, stationery and the like) are for the bestowal of relief and charities of the needy . . . we will take judicial notice, that the grand and subordinate lodges of freemasons within the state of Alabama constitute a charitable or eleemosynary corporation.

In The People v. Rockford Masonic Temple Building Association, 181 N. E. 428 (1932), 348 Ill. 567, the court said on page 569:

> From the evidence it is apparent that the primary purpose and object of the various organizations which use the building is to promulgate the ideals of Masonry, which include the maintenance of a high moral standard of living and administration to the religious and spiritual life of its members.

In Ancient Accepted Scottish Rite v. Board of County Commissioners, 122 Neb. 586, 241 N. W. 93 (1932), the court said on page 591 to 592:

> Masonry is traditionally and generally described as a system of morality veiled in allegory and illustrated by symbols. It teaches as a foundation principle faith in God and immortality of the soul. Masonry is not sectarian in its religious teaching. It aims to bring devotees a deeper and more conscious contact with spiritual things. To the extent that religious purposes include the field of morals, Masonry makes common cause with organized religion. Masonry is tolerant of all faiths and builds a moral and spiritual fellowship on the foundations of fundamental morality common to them. It

brings its members to the altar of prayer, and by its very teachings and effort seeks to make real the invisible power of love, the intrinsic worth of harmony, and the beauty and eternal reality of the ideal. Outside of the activity of Masonry which is devoted to charity, which constitutes a very substantial part and major part of its endeavors, all of its activities in all its bodies are devoted to these purposes which fall within the definition of 'education' and 'religion'.

In Strickland v. Prichard, 37 Vt. 324 (1864) it is noted a Royal Arch Chapter disposed of its assets in 1836, apparently as a result of the antimasonic political movement, Years later members of the Chapter filed suit to recover the assets. The court observed (p. 236) that during a period of our history there was a great deal of distrust and hostility towards the Craft and this became the dominant element of one of the political parties in the state. Consequently the legislature passed a number of laws designed to destroy Freemasonry. The court then said:

> Whether the institution deserved all or any of its censure and unpopularity which it then suffered, we have now but insufficient means of knowing, and perhaps it would hardly be just to accept the legislative indications of those few years as establishing a general legal policy upon the subject.

The court held against the plaintiffs on the ground that they were new members, a new group, and had no legal claim to the assets of the prior Chapter.

In Morrow v. Smith, 145 Iowa 514 (1910), the court said on page 523:

> . . . a very substantial part of the activity of this order is devoted to the help of those who are needy and in distress. Granted that its benevolence is principally confined to those within its immediate circle, it is nevertheless commendable as far as it goes, and in the interest of the public good. It could not, if it would, take care of all destitution. If it does all that it can, it does well; and, if it expends what it has upon those whose need it knows best, so be it. In some such wise must all ministry be done. The testator was a member of this particular lodge for many years. He was said to be charitable in his own nature, and was greatly interested in the charities of his order. Through the instrumentalities of his lodge he desired to continue his benevolences for the future. That he regarded the order as a charitable institution in its relation to his bequest is manifest.

It must be noted that Freemasonry no longer confines its charitable endeavors to its own members. Over two million dollars a day is spent by Freemasonry to help, aid and assist the dIstressed. Most of this money is distributed outside the fraternity.

In United Grand Lodge of Ancient Free and Accepted Masons of England v. Holborn Borough Council, 3 All E. R. 281 (1957), 121 J. P. 595, 101 Sol. J. 851, the court considered the question of whether Freemasons Hall in London was to be taxed at a rate covering non-profit organizations "concerned with the advancement of religion." The court on page 284 said:

> Masons are charged to be good citizens, to work honestly, to act as moral and wise men, to relieve a brother Mason in want in preference to other poor, and to cultivate brotherly love, 'so that all may see the benign influence of Masonry'.

In deciding that Freemasonry does not advance religion, the court said on page 285:

> To advance religion means to promote it, to spread its message ever wider among mankind; to take some positive steps to sustain and increase religious belief; and these things are done in a variety of ways which may be comprehensively described as pastoral and missionary. There is nothing comparable to that in Masonry. This is not said by way of criticism. For Masonry really does something different. It says to a man, "Whatever your religion or mode of worship, believe in a Supreme Creator and lead a good moral life." Laudable as this precept is, it does not appear to us to be the same thing as the advancement of religion. There is no religious instruction, no programme for the persuasion of unbelievers, no religious supervision to see that the members remain active and constant in the various religions they profess, no holding of religious services, no pastoral or missionary work of any kind.

In M. W. Widow's Sons Grand Lodge v. M. W. Prince Hall Grand Lodge, 160 Pa. Super. 595, 52 Atl. 2d 334 (1947), two rival black groups, calling themselves "Masonic," engaged in a proceeding in which the Prince Hall Organization opposed the issuance of a state charter to the other group claiming there was a confusing similarity of names. The court said on page 334:

THE COURTS AND FREEMASONRY

Fraternal orders or lodges exist in great number and variety in our country, and many of them possess the public esteem because of the integrity and good works practiced by them through the years. Their purposes are benign and their objects worthy. They emphasize man's duty to live as a human, social and unselfish being, and seek to discourage his living unto himself alone. Such fraternities are woven inextricably into the weft and warp of the web of society. Their members are drawn from all walks of life and schools of thought, and they are characteristically democratic institutions. They therefore do not do well, nor long survive, in totalitarian countries, in which usually the first move of the dictator is to abolish both church and fraternal societies, for each emphasizes the individual dignity and liberty of men. They are therefore entitled to the careful solicitude of law and her courts.

The principles hereinafter enunciated apply not only to the fraternity now involved but to all fraternal organizations.

In Mason v. Zimmerman, 81 Kan. 799, 106 Pac. 1005 (1910), the court, on appeal, observed that the following findings of fact had been made by the trial court (pp. 1006-1007):

(2) Said Grand Lodge of Masons is an association of persons who are or have been the principal officers of the subordinate lodges of Ancient, Free and Accepted Masons of the state, who meet in annual convention for the transaction of business affairs of such Grand Lodge. The Plaintiffs are the four principal officers of such Grand Lodge constituting what is known as the "Council of Administration". The Grand Secretary is also elected at the annual meeting of the Grand Lodge, has an office in the building on the premises in question, and attends to the routine business of the lodge. The Grand Lodge has general supervision and control of the affairs of the subordinate or local Masonic lodges of the state.

(3) The order of Ancient, Free and Accepted Masons is an association of persons that has existed for several hundred years, and exists generally in all civilized countries. In the state of Kansas there are 379 local or subordinate lodges, organized under the supervision and direction of said Grand Lodge, and subject to its jurisdiction. The lodges of this state are independent and separate from those of any other state or country, except that all Masonic lodges are bound by cer-

tain ancient landmarks and principles, which are not subject to change by either a subordinate or grand lodge. The objects and purposes of the Masonic order and of the Masonic lodges of Kansas are to inculcate in their members the principles of morality, temperance, benevolence, and charity, and teach them their duty to one another and to all mankind; to care for the sick and afflicted; to relieve the wants of the needy and destitute; and to promote the general good and welfare and orphans of such members. None of such lodges are, nor are permitted to engage in any business for profit, nor is there connected with them any sick or death benefits, to which such members are entitled by reason of any consideration given by such member to secure the same, the care of the sick and help of the needy being actuated by purely charitable and benevolent motives, without return or compensation. Under the rule of the order each subordinate Masonic lodge pays annually into the treasury of the Grand Lodge a sum equal to $1 for each member. In addition to such contribution, each subordinate lodge, through its committee on charity, which each lodge is required to have, makes contributions for the care of the sick and the help of the needy, as circumstances may require, generally among its own members and other Masons and their families, but not exclusively so. Such lodges are, as a rule, supported wholly by annual dues paid by their members, and the monies so received are devoted wholly to current expenses and to charitable and benevolent purposes.

(4) The functions of the Grand Lodge are, for the most part, of an administrative character. . . .

In Scottish Rite Building Company v. Lancaster County, 106 Neb. 95, 184 N. W. 574 (1921), in considering whether the Masonic Order serves "religious purposes" the court said on page 102 to 105:

The evidence show that belief in and reverence for a Supreme Being are required of each and every member; that it makes no difference whether that Supreme Being is 'God' or 'Allah'; that belief in Christianity is not exacted, and that people may belong who do not believe in the divinity of Christ. The fact that belief in the doctrines or deity of no particular religion is required, of itself, refutes the theory that the Masonic ritual embodies a religion, or that its teachings are religious. It is conceivable that the Scottish Rite bodies, or the Masonic order generally, set themselves up as exponents of a new religion? For if they belong to none of the old established religions, and yet assume to preach or expound religion, they must be embarking upon a new theology and setting up a religion of their own.

The true interpretation of the Masonic attitude in that respect is that no religious test at all is applied as a condition of membership. The guiding thought is not religion but religious toleration. The order simply exacts of its members that they shall not be atheists and deny the existence of God or Supreme Being. Each member is encouraged to pay due reverence to his own God, the Deity prescribed by his own religion, and to obey those precepts of human conduct, which, while taught by all religions prevalent in civilized society, do not appertain to the mysteries or doctrines of any religion, as such, but are common to all. The Masonic fraternity, in other words, refrains from intruding into the field of religion and confines itself to the teachings of morality and duty to one's fellow men, which makes them better men and better citizens.

The distinction is clear between such ethical teachings and the doctrines of religion. One cannot espouse a religion without belief and faith in its peculiar doctrines. If a Christian, for instance, one must believe in the divine mission and revelation of the Saviour, with all that is implied and included therein; if a Mohammedan, one must believe in the revelation of the doctrine of that religion through the Koran, of which Mohammed was the prophet. A fraternity, however, broad enough to take in and cover with its mantle Christian, Moslem, and Jew, without requiring either to renounce his religion, is not a religious organization, although its members may join in prayer which, in the case of each, is a petition in the immortality of the soul be denominated religious, in the sense that it is typical of all religions, of any race, or of any age. It constitutes, to be sure, one of the most beautiful and consolatory features of our own religion, but it is equally to be found in almost every other. It is so universal and spontaneous that it is not so much a belief or dogma as it is an instinct of the human soul. Neither does it imply or require adherence to any system of religious worship; many pagan and infidel philosophers have asserted it. It is so generally subscribed to by everybody that it does not run counter to any one's religious belief, and, as in the case of belief in the Supreme Being, the profession of belief in the immortality of the soul does not create any religious division among the members of the Masonic order.

It cannot but occur to the thoughtful mind that in putting forward the resemblance of its ceremonies to the observances of religious worship, and in claiming the right to exemption for its property from taxation upon that ground, counsel have assumed a position which, when carried to its final analysis, would, if sustained, go farther than the order itself has clearly contemplated and would lead to results harmful and impracticable. For the Scottish Rite bodies to be pronounced by law, or court decision, religious organizations would mean that their meetings must be construed to be the equivalent of divine worship, and their officiating officers to be clergymen or ministers—of what gospel, it is impossible to say. Owing to the perfect liberty of conscience which people of every religious faith enjoy under our institutions, it has become a marked characteristic of religious worship in this country that it should be held in public and with open doors. It would be an anomaly, to say the least, if it should become the practice to give religious sanction to the meetings of secret societies and to rites and services carried on in the guise of religious worship to which the public would be denied admission.

The fact that they display in their ceremonies a becoming reverence for the Deity and strive to inculcate the principles of morality does not change the essentially temporal or secular character of the Scottish Rite bodies, or clothe them with the spiritual or sacred attributes of a religious or ecclesiastical institution, any more than the custom of family prayers, or of religious or moral instruction in the home would have that result. . . . The evidence will not bear out the assumption that the ceremonies in question are religious rites or services.

II. THE MASONIC ORGANIZATION

2.1 Legal Existence of Organization.

There is a legal distinction between the various persons who are members of an association and the organization itself. This distinction in the law is described, for convenience, as a difference in entities. It has been stated that only persons can act or engage in activities. The law classifies persons into two general groups (1) Natural persons and (2) Artificial persons. The second classification includes such groups as corporations and other entities recognized by law. In Department of Banking v. Hedges, 136 Neb. 382, 286 N. W. 277 (1939), the court said on page 281: "The word 'entity' means a real being in existence. 'Legal entity,' therefore, means legal existence. The subject is discussed generally in 7 C. J. S. page 22 to 30 and 36 Am. Juris. page 814.

This subject is more than one of academic interest. It becomes of vital importance in the area of owning real estate, taking gifts under a will, the filing of suits, and other areas. Here are some illustrative cases where the subject became vital.

In Marsh River Lodge v. Brook, 61 Me. 585 (1873), members of a Masonic Lodge, which was organized as a voluntary association, secured a charter with the name "The Marsh River Corporation". Suit was filed in the name of the lodge, then the plaintiff asked to substitute the name of the corporation as the plaintiff. The court held this could not be done, saying on page 587 "A voluntary unincorporated association and a corporation duly organized under the laws of the State, cannot be regarded as identical."

In Re Rathbone's Will, 11 N. Y. S. 2d 506, affirmed in 287 N. Y. 708, 39 N. E. 2d 930 (1942), the will made certain bequests to a Shrine Temple, a Commandery, a Scottish Rite body, a Lodge, and to the Masonic Home of Pennsylvania. All the bequests were held to be void except the ones to the Lodge and to the Masonic Home. The basis for the decision was that the other bodies were not legal entities and therefore had no legal existence. But later the law was changed and the result was different. See Wiley's Estate, 136 N. Y. S. 2d 309 (1954).

In the following cases the court held that under local state law Masonic bodies were entities and were entitled to receive bequests made under a will. Collins v. Russell, 115 F. 2d 334 (1940); Clark v. Watkins, 130 Kan. 549, 287 Pac 244 (1930).

Mason v. Finch, 28 Mich 282 (1873), was a suit to recover personal property claimed by a Royal Arch Chapter. There had existed an unincorporated society, but later a corporation was formed with the same name. The court held that even an absolute identity of the members would not merge the two groups. Both groups were held to be separate and not the same.

In Magness v. Chicora Chapter, 193 S. C. 205, 8 S. E. 2d 344 (1940), it was held that the incorporation of the Grand Chapter of Royal Arch Masons did not have the effect of incorporating each subordinate Chapter. But, Burdine v. Grand Lodge of Alabama, 37 Ala. 478 (1861), held that the incorporation of the Grand Lodge had the effect of incorporating the constituent Lodges.

In Brooks v. Owen, 200 Iowa 1151, 202 N. W. 505 (1925), two Masonic bodies, that were voluntary associations, were sued and a judgement was entered against them. The defendants then urged, for the first time, that they were not legal entities and therefore could not be sued. The court held that the objection came too late.

In Cruse v. Axtell, 50 Ind. 49 (1875), a will left certain real estate to a Masonic Lodge and appointed trustees to handle the details. The objectors claimed that the Lodge was not a legal entity, and therefore, could not take under the will. The court held that the Lodge was a quasi corporation, or a corporation de facto, or an organization of persons having a name and was sufficiently identified and could take under the will.

The above problems are not likely to arise today as most Masonic groups are legal entities of one kind or another. For example, in Polar Star Lodge v. Polar Star Lodge, 16 La. Ann. 53 (1861), the legislature of the state, in 1819 by a special statute, created the Grand Lodge of Louisiana and granted permission to create constituent Lodges which thereby became separate entities.

In Collins v. Russell, 114 Fed. 2d 334 (1940), the statute had a long list of organizations which were authorized to hold real estate in their own names. It did not list specifically the Knights Templar group. In construing the statute the court held that the Knights Templar organization came under the general provision covering lodges with charters from fraternal, benevolent or charitable lodges.

2.2 Majority of Members Cannot Dissolve Group.

The members of an association and the association, as such, are separate and apart and occupy the same position as two different persons. Therefore, their rights are not identical. The question sometimes arises whether a majority of the members of an association can dissolve it by a vote. This will depend, in part, on the rules of the association and other factors. The general rule is set forth in 7 C. J. S. (1980) as follows:

> An association may be dissolved by its own action taken in accordance with the articles of association or by-laws, by unanimous vote of its members, or by abandonment of non-

user of the association.

Here are a few illustrative Masonic cases:

In Polar Star Lodge No. 1 v. Polar Star Lodge No. 1, 16 La. Ann. 53 (1891), the Lodge had been formed in 1819, but in 1855, a majority of the members adopted a resolution to dissolve the Lodge. They secured a new charter and claimed the property of the original Lodge. The court stated that the resolution was invalid. So long as there were enough members in the group to conduct the affairs of the Lodge it would continue to exist. Therefore, the new Lodge was not entitled to the property of the original Lodge.

In Curien v. Santini, 16 La. Ann 27 (1861), the legislature had created the Grand Lodge and authorized it to issue charters creating subordinate Lodges. After a Lodge received a charter from the Grand Lodge, forty-three out of fifty members, adopted a resolution to dissolve the Lodge. The court held that the resolution did not have the effect of dissolving the Lodge and that it could continue to exist as long as there were members to carry on its affairs.

In Smith v. Smith, 3 Dess. 559 (1817, S. C.), the officers of the "Modern" Grand Lodge and of the "Ancient" Grand Lodge met, settled their differences, and decided to unite by forming another Grand Lodge as a "voluntary association". In implementing the settlement certain disagreements arose and suit was filed by the new group to secure the funds of one of the original groups. The court in a long and detailed opinion considered the Landmarks of the Craft, as well as other authorities, and concluded on the basis of general rules of law, that the plaintiffs had no standing in court. That the original group was still in existence, and that the new group was not entitled to the funds.

In Plemenik v. Prickett, 97 N. J. Eq. 310 (1924), Schiller Lodge had worked in the German language for years, but, with the coming of World War One the Grand Lodge adopted a rule that all work in its Lodges had to be in the English language. When the war was over the members of Schiller Lodge requested that they be permitted to resume work in the German language and this was refused. The Lodge, nevertheless, resumed work in the German language and the Grand Lodge arrested its charter. In this case the court held that this action was proper, but, this was not the end of the matter. In United States Savings Bank of Newark v. Schiller Lodge, 117 N. J. Eq. 460, 176 Atl. 330 (1935), the court held that in view of the action of the Grand Lodge the funds and property of a dissolved Lodge went to the Grand Lodge even though the bulk of the members of the original Lodge had resigned and formed another Lodge.

2.3 Association Can Only Act Within Powers Granted.

The general rule is that associations may do all things necessary to accomplish the purpose of their existence. Sometimes statutes grant powers specifically to associations and sometimes powers are granted in the charters creating the association. Powers may also be stated in state constitutional provisions. Powers possessed by the officers of the association may be set forth in the constitution and by-laws of the association (7 C. J. S. 79; 1980). Since some associations are not considered legal entities (as explained above) they cannot hold property in their names, sue or be sued in the name of the association (6 Am. Juris. 2d 438; 36 Am. Juris. 2d 826). If the association does anything outside the scope of its authority the acts are not valid or binding (36 Am. Juris. 2d 829). Here are some illustrations of cases applying these rules.

In Grand Lodge of Alabama v. Waddill, 36 Ala. 313 (1860), the court held that the Grand Lodge could not recover in the suit based on a note signed by the defendants when money was loaned to them to be used by the Central Masonic Institute. The court applied the well established rule that a corporation can only do those things which it is authorized to do by its charter, and that in this instance no authority was given to the Grand Lodge to make loans of money. Therefore, it could not recover in the suit.

In the case entitled In re Monroe Chapter No. 57, Order of the Eastern Star, 132 Mis. 109, 228 N. Y. S. 248 (1927), a mandamus suit was filed requesting the court to enter an order directing that a charter be restored and that suspended members also be re-instated. There had been a dispute over an assessment of twenty-five cents a member and the members of the chapter refused to pay the assessment. The court held that the Grand Chapter had no power to levy the assessment and ordered that the chapter be restored and the members be re-instated.

In Washbon v. Hixon, 87 Kans. 310, 124 Pac. 366 (1912), the court held that a Grand Lodge check that was used to pay a personal obligation of an officer was improperly issued without authority and that the money could be recovered in this suit.

In Halcyon Lodge v. Watson, 7 Kans. 661, 53 Pac. 879 (1898), suit was filed against the Lodge to recover for nursing care supplied a sick member. The court held the plaintiff could not recover as the persons who ordered the services to be rendered were not authorized to bind the Lodge and there had never been a vote of the Lodge to incur the obligation or that said obligation was later ratified by the Lodge.

In State v. Toney, 141 Ore. 406, 17 P. 2d 1105 (1933), the Grand Lodge adopted a resolution to use part of the funds in the educational fund to meet some expenses of the home endowment fund. The court said on page 1106:

> The protection of quasi public charities and trusts is peculiarly within the inherent power of a court of equity. These powers are always available to compel the trustees of such trusts to discharge their duties according to the conditions under which they were held.

The court also said on page 1106 and 1107:

> The charitable uses designated by the donor of a fund cannot be changed to any other purpose so long as there are objects of such charity or so long as it can be applied to the purpose named.

2.4 Right to Exclusive Use of Name.

Associations usually adopt a name by which they can be identified. Sometimes associations also adopt emblems and regalia which are associated with the group by non-members. The general rule on this subject appears in 6 Am. Juris. 2d 442 and is as follows:

> The prevailing doctrine is that an unincorporated benevolent, fraternal, or social organization is entitled to protection against the use of its name by another organization, and may resort to injunctive relief to restrain the use of its name by others, unless the right is lost by acquiescence and laches. In this connection it has been held that such an organization is not entitled to protection in the use of its name in the absence of a showing of pecuniary injury, although there is authority to the contrary. In any event, an association cannot restrain another organization from using words from a part

of its name which are not subject to exclusive appropriation, or restrain the use of a name assumed by another which is sufficiently different to prevent anyone from being misled.

See also: 7 C. J. S. 81 and 10 C. J. S. 256.

Here are some illustrative cases:

In Grand Orient Lodge of Louisiana v. Jackson, 12 La. App. 555 (1930), suit was filed by Le Grand Orient de la Louisiane for an injunction against the Grand Orient Lodge claiming confusion resulting from the similarity of the names. The court noted that the plaintiff had been in existence and using the name for many years. The court issued the injunction (p. 556) and held that the use of the name by the defendant was "an infringement of the rights of the prior user for any one else to adopt similar words with a Masonic brother fraternal organization."

In Faisan v. Adair, 144 Ga. 797, 87 S. E. 1080 (1915), an injunction suit was filed by the Shrine Temple in Atlanta against the Shrine group consisting of black men which used the same name as the plaintiff, except, that it added the word "Egyptian" between the words "Ancient" and "Arabic" and they also used similar regalia and emblems. The court held that the injunction against the defendants was proper since the similarities were misleading. The court observed that the fact that the two groups drew their membership from different races and did not mix socially and fraternally was not sufficient ground for denying injunctive relief.

In Burrell v. Michaux, 279 U. S. 737 (1929), a similar suit was filed in Texas and the plaintiff won in the trial court and in the Supreme Court of Texas. But the United States Supreme Court reversed the decision on the ground that the plaintiff had waited too long before filing suit. This is in accord with the general rule that one who has a legal or equitable right must urge it promptly and if he waits too long it amounts to consent and the complaint comes too late. In this case there was a delay of eighteen years before suit was filed. Another defense urged by the defendant was that there was no confusion because one group restricted its membership to white men and the other to black men.

These cases are always based on the contention that the names of the two organizations are so similar that they cause confusion in the minds of the general public and prospective members. Sometimes there is the added element of fraudulent oral representation as the new organization campaigns to secure members.

Over the years successful fraternal organizations of all kinds have been plagued with imitators. There are a large number of reported cases involving various fraternal groups in which injunctions were sought to stop the competition and resulting confusion that results from the use of similar names, emblems, etc. There are a number of cases in which the organizations were formed by black persons using the word "Masonic" in their names. Theses groups have been operating for years outside the mainstream of the regular Craft, and one group did possess a charter for a few years from the Grand Lodge of England and they try to justify their existence with this element. These groups are outside the scope of our interest here but the subject is mentioned merely as a matter of academic interest. In the appendix to this book there is listed reported cases of such black organizations for the guidance of our readers who may be interested in this subject. A number of these cases, however, present some interesting facets and are presented here.

Most of these cases, involving black persons, went on the proposition of whether the similarity in the names was misleading to the public. The cases were usually decided on which group was organized first, appeared in the area first, and whether the second group was acting in a fraudulent manner. The matter of "legitimacy" of one of the groups was seldom discussed by the court. As a matter of fact, in Grand Lodge v. Grimshaw, 34 D. of C. App. 383 (1910), a suit was filed by a black group to restrain another black group from operating as a Masonic Lodge. The defendant filed a cross-complaint for the same relief and the prayer of the defendant was allowed by the trial court. There was an appeal of the decision and the court observed that there was no evidence that any person desiring to become a Mason was deceived by the similarity of the two names of the organizations involved and held that dismissing the complaint was correct but that granting an injunction on the cross-complaint was improper. The court said on page 385:

> Courts of equity do not exercise jurisdiction to inquire into or adjudicate the right of different associations for charitable or religious objects to hold themselves out to be the regular and only accredited representatives of some particular order or religious system.

Undoubtedly, the court felt it was sufficiently informed in the matter and felt it was not qualified to pass on the matter of which of the two groups were entitled to be considered "legitimate."

The matter becomes a bit muddled because in the 1800's representatives of the Prince Hall Organization met in a Convention and formed a National, or, Compact Grand Lodge. Within a few years some of the lodges withdrew from this new group, but, it continued to exist and has issued charters up to the present time. On the basis of the element of claimed "legitimate origin" lodges chartered by the National, or, Compact Lodge are no more or no less legitimate than the Prince Hall lodges, because they both trace their origin to African Lodge No. 457. Yet, the Prince Hall Organization ignores these lodges, considers them irregular, and on occasion has filed suits against them. One such case is M. W. United Grand Lodge v. Green, 136 Md. 582, 110 Atl. 851 (1920).

In Colorado, some years ago, an unusual thing took place which is worthy of note. In. M. W. Prince Hall Grand Lodge v. M. W. Hiram Grand Lodge, 85 Colo. 17, 273 Pac. 648 (1928), suit was filed by the Prince Hall Organization against the National Compact Prince Hall Origin Grand Lodge. The court on appeal reversed the decision of the trial court and sent the case back to the trial court for further action. When the case reached the trial court the regular Masonic organization, consisting of white persons, filed an intervening petition and asked to be heard. The original defendant lost interest in the controversy and withdrew from the case leaving the Prince Hall Organization and the regular Masonic organization in the case to litigate. In 86 Colo. 330, 282 Pac. 193 (1929), which was an appeal from the decision of the trial court in the dispute between the regular Grand Lodge and the Prince Hall Organization, the court held that the regular Masonic Grand Lodge had the exclusive right to use the name "Masonic" and enjoined the Prince Hall Grand Lodge from using the term. In a strict legal sense, the Prince Hall Organization and the other black groups using the word "Masonic" have been doing so by sufferance of the regular Masonic organization.

This subject has been considered so important by the Prince Hall Organization that two books have been published to assist attorneys in filing suit against competitors. One book is by Amos T. Hall and the other by George W. Crawford. Both books are entitled *The Prince Hall Counselor.*

In M. W. Grand Lodge v. M. W. Prince Hall Grand Lodge, 90 W. Va. 424, 111 S. E. 309 (1922), a schism existed in which a number of black persons withdrew from the "Masonic organization." A number of persons who withdrew met at a convention and formed a new group and took steps to secure a charter from the State with the name "Most Worshipful Prince Hall Grand Lodge of West Virginia, A. F. & A. M."

Suit was filed by the original group to enjoin the use of part of the names of this new group. The court held that on the basis of the evidence presented it was not shown that there was any confusion in the use of the names of the two groups, there was no deception used by the new group, that the words in the name were truly descriptive of the work of the two groups, that the work of both was worthy, and that the court should not grant a monopoly to either group in the use of the name.

The doctrine of "exclusive jurisdiction" is anathema to the Prince Hall Organization when it is observed that the regular organization states that only one Grand Lodge is considered "regular" in each state of the United States. And yet in two cases where black "Masonic" organizations were litigating which was entitled to have the exclusive right to exist, the doctrine was urged upon the court (M. W. Grand Lodge v. West Temple Lodge, 47 Ariz. 57, 53 Pac. 2d 435, 1936; M. W. Hiram of Tyre Grand Lodge v. M. W. Sons of Light Grand Lodge, 94 Cal. App. 2d 25, 210 Pac. 2d 34, 1949).

For further information on this subject see *A Documentary Account of Prince Hall and other Black Fraternal orders* by H. W. Coil, Sr.; John M. Sherman and Harold V. B. Voorhis, 1982, Missouri Lodge of Research.

2.5 Irregular Groups.

Each Grand Lodge has the power to decide what other groups are to be recognized as being "regular." Several cases on this subject are of interest to us.

In Bayliss v. Grand Lodge of Louisiana, 131 La. 579, 59 So. 996 (1912), the plaintiff filed suit for damages claimed to have been sustained by him as a result of the Grand Lodge labeling him as a seller of spurious degrees. This is a famous case with a long and detailed opinion by the court and the decision against Bayliss rang the death toll of the Cerneau controversy in the United States after many years of confusion.

In Bergera v. U. S., 297 Fed. 102 (1924), the defendants, by using an irregular organization, had been convicted of using the mail to sell Masonic degrees. For years, Matthew McBain Thomson, had engaged in extensive promotion and the sale of claimed Masonic degrees through his American Masonic Federation and the Confederated Supreme Council. The defendants were found guilty of using the mail to defraud. The details of this interesting case are presented in a book written in 1922, by Isaac Blair Evans, entitled "The Thomson Masonic Fraud."

As already noted in two cases involving black organizations, the court declined to pass on the matter of regularity of two contending groups (M. W. Grand Lodge of the District of Columbia v. Grimshaw, 34 App. D. C. 383, 1910 and M. W. United Grand Lodge v. Green, 136 Md. 582, 110 Atl. 851, 1920).

2.6 Liability of Non-Member Using Emblem of Group.

In certain states there are statutes that make it illegal for a non-member to wear the emblem of an organization. The general rule on this subject is stated in 6 Am. Juris. 2d 443 as follows:

> A state legislature may, under its police power, forbid persons who are not members of secret societies from wearing or using the badges or emblems belonging to such societies. No Constitutional privilege or immunities are denied a citizen, nor are exclusive privileges or preferences unlawfully conferred or given, by such legislation.

The leading case on this subject is Hammer v. State, 173 Ind. 199, 89 N. E. 850 (1909), and the court stated as follows on page 203 in commenting on the constitutional aspects of the matter:

> It can be scarcely be urged that the right to wear a badge or emblem of a society of which a person is not a member is a right conferred by the Constitution or laws of the United States. The statute confers no right, exemption or privilege on any class or individual to do a thing denied to others as of common right, except it may be said negatively to authorize one who is a member of the society to wear a badge if he chooses, but prevents all who are not members from doing so. The Constitution and laws of the United States do not furnish, nor guarantee such right, nor can a person under them claim that right as a privilege, or that he shall be immune from regulation by the State, so far as the federal Constitution is concerned. It is simply the denial by the State, under its police power, of a claim of right by appellant. It is the negation of a claim, and is a matter that concerns the State only.

In discussing the logical justification for the prohibition the court said on page 205 to 206:

> It is a matter of common knowledge that the membership in most, if not all, societies or organizations, whether secret or otherwise, is the result of fitness and selection, which gives members standing and character, at least among their fellows, and to a greater or lesser degree with the public, and he who wears a badge or emblem of the order or society without being a member holds himself out to the public and to actual members as guilty of a false personation. It is of

itself a deceit and a false pretense, and its object could be nothing else than deception, with possible ulterior motives. It is evidence of the first act of an impostor in the course of a premeditated design to prey upon those who, from fraternal, charitable or sympathetic motives, become the victims of false personation, imposition and fraud, whether members of the society or not, and the object of the statute was the prevention of this species of fraud, not only in the interest of the members of the society, but of the public at large, who might be deceived through their good opinion of the society and its members. It is a police regulation, pure and simple, upon grounds of public policy, directed against false personation and false pretenses of that particular kind. False pretenses need not be in words. At common law, 'cheats,' not amounting to a felony, are such as are effected by deceitful or illegal symbols or tokens which may affect the public at large, and against which common prudence could not have guarded, to the injury of one in some pecuniary interest.

This is not an isolated case on this subject. Other cases holding to the same effect are—State v. Holland, 37 Mont. 393, 96 Pac. 719 (1908); Commonwealth v. Martin, 35 Pa. Super. 241 (1908) and State v. Turner, 182 Kans. 496, 328 Pac. 2d 733 (1958). In the Montana case the court held the specific statute invalid because it exempted from its provisions the female relatives of members and the court held this was improper. Later the statute was re-enacted without this exception.

This subject is discussed in 13 Royal Arch Mason Magazine 264 (Spring, 1981).

2.7 Grand Lodge Rights and Powers.

On the organizational level, under Masonic law, the Grand Lodge which has issued the charter creating the lodge is supreme. It occupies an unusual position since the persons who compose the Grand Lodge are generally elected officers of the constituent lodges. When the Grand Lodge is meeting as such, it has administrative, judicial, and legislative power. The general rules relating to the relationship between the Grand Lodge and the lodges chartered by it are discussed in 36 Am. Juris. 2d 833 et seq. These rules may be summarized as follows:

"The constitution and bylaws of the central governing body of a fraternal benefit society generally determine its relations to the various subordinate divisions of the organization" (36 Am. Jurs. 2d 833).

"The superior body is usually the sole judge of the election and qualification of its own officers and members, and the rights of different persons claiming to represent a subordinate lodge of an order are to be determined by the constitution and bylaws of the grand lodge" (36 Am Juris. 2d 834).

"All the subdivisions of an order derive their powers from the central or governing body and are subject to its authority" (36 C. J. S. 2d 835).

"Generally, the supreme or parent governing body of a fraternal order . . . operating on the lodge system, has . . . authority to suspend or expel subordinate lodges or branches in proper cases, upon compliance with such conditions precedent as may be deemed necessary to protect the rights of such branches and their members" (36 C. J. S. 2d 837).

". . . There is authority to the effect that it is the duty of the supreme lodge, upon suspending a subordinate lodge which has members in good standing, to make proper provision for such members by notifying them individually of the suspension, and . . . affording them an opportunity to join another lodge in good standing" (36 Am. Juris. 2d 838).

"A fraternal order . . . is formed by the purely voluntary association of individuals for the accomplishment of such objects as they have mutually agreed on, and as the selection of the purposes for which the association is established and the determination of the means by which these purposes shall be accomplished are peculiarly matters to be decided by the association alone, it is generally acknowledged that within their own field they are supreme in matters of discipline and internal policy not manifestly involving private rights, and that the members of such association can undoubtedly restrict themselves as to matters incidental to the operation of the association to remedies before the tribunal created by it" (36 Am. Juris. 2d 841).

In 94 A. L. R. 639 et seq, there appears a detailed discussion of the subject "Expulsion or Suspension of local Lodge or other unit of a Benefit Society."

In Bayliss v. Grand Lodge, 131 La. 579, 59 So. 996 (1912), involving a Cerneau group, the court said on page 606 to 607:

> It is clear that, as between itself and its constituents (the Blue Lodge and the members thereof), the Grand Lodge was within its rights in enacting the law which we have referred, for the Grand Lodge is a legislative body, created by, and of those constituents, and the law in question was made by

them, through their representatives, to be applied to themselves.

2.8 Business Activities of Organizations.

There have been times when Masonic lodges and other Masonic groups have engaged in a business activity. When they do this the groups become subject to the usual rules pertaining to such transactions. Here are some illustrative cases relating to such matters.

In Fairmont Lodge No. 590 v. Tilton, 122 Ill. App. 636 (1905), the lodge rented the second floor of a building. The premises were in disrepair and it became necessary to spend a substantial amount of money to repair the roof. The court, applying general rules of law, held that although a lessor is not bound to make repairs to the premises unless the lease so provides, the rule of law is otherwise when only a part of the premises are rented. In such instances there is a duty on the part of the lessor to make repairs to that part of the premises that involves all the tenants such as the roof, halls and other common elements.

In McClellan v. Robe, 93 Ind. 298 (1883), suit was filed on a note, in usual form, signed by five persons with the following words added after their names "Trustees of the Greenwood Lodge No. 192, F. and A. M." The court held that the persons who signed were liable and that the words added after their names did not make the note that of the lodge.

In Masonic Temple Safety Deposit Co. v. Langfelt, 117 Ill. App. 652 (1905), suit was filed claiming damages for money permitted to be taken from a safety deposit box by a person not authorized to have access to the boxes that were located in a Masonic Temple. The court affirmed the decision of the jury holding that the defendant was negligent.

When Masonic groups decide to buy or rent real estate they become subject to the general rules of law pertaining to these relationships. Here are a few illustrative cases of this type of situation.

The Great Masonic Temple, some years after it was erected in Chicago around 1890, was subjected to litigation by the city to make major changes in the assembly halls and stairways. Here, the problem is whether a city can require a property owner to make changes in the structure after the building has been erected with the approval of the city. Masonic Fraternity Temple Association v. City of Chicago, 217 Ill. 58, 75 N. E. 439 (1905); 120 Ill. App. 612 and 131 Ill. App. 1.

In Great Atlantic & PACIFIC Tea Co. v. Athens Lodge No. 165, 207 S. W. 2d 217 (Tex., 1947), the lodge sought to evict a tenant who claimed it had a lease signed by the secretary of the Lodge. The court held that the lease was invalid because it was not authorized by the Lodge and the acceptance of rent by the Lodge did not amount to a ratification of the lease in the hands of the tenant.

In Ashbury v. Hugh L. Bates Lodge No. 686, 62 Ohio App. 430, 24 N. E. 2d 638 (1939), five lodge members offered to sell a lot to the Lodge. The Lodge passed a resolution authorizing the Master and Wardens to purchase the property and nothing further was done in the matter. A suit was filed to compel the Lodge to complete the purchase. The court held that the minutes of the meeting did not comply with the general rule that all contracts for the sale of real estate must be in writing and signed by the parties to the contract.

In Rhodes v. Maret, 112 S. W. 433 (Tex. Civ. App., 1908), suit was filed by the Lodge to secure possession of real estate. The Lodge and the community of Acton had entered into a written agreement to erect a building to be occupied as a school and as a Lodge hall. The agreement had been signed by many of its members, but, not by the Lodge. From 1866 to 1870 the community hired a teacher and paid the school expenses. In 1905 the school district broke into the building and put it to use. The court held that the Lodge was a trustee of the property and that adverse possession did not apply in the matter.

In Reynolds v. St. John's Grand Lodge, 171 La. 395, 131 So. 186 (1930), the Grand Lodge paid a mortgage on the Lodge's real estate and title to the property was conveyed to the Grand Lodge. Some members of the Lodge filed suit to invalidate the transfer and the court held that the transfer was valid.

In Rome v. New River Lodge No. 402, 197 So. 174 (La. Appl, 1940), a dispute arose between the Lodge and an adjoining owner regarding a claimed encroachment of the Lodge building on the adjoining land. The matter was settled by giving the Lodge a ninety-nine year lease with rent at one dollar a year. Later the adjoining owner filed suit to cancel the lease claiming fraud because the Lodge permitted soft drinks, candy, and cigarettes to be sold on its premises. The court held in favor of the Lodge on the basis of the evidence presented.

In Columbia Lodge No. 82 v. Peace, 197 Ark. 1175, 128 S. W. 2d 266 (1939), the Lodge rented space to a tenant who paid two months rent and then stated that the lease was void because the committee of the Lodge had no authority to act. The court held that the tenant, having accepted the benefits of the lease, and the rent having been accepted by the Lodge, this constituted a ratification of the lease and therefore was binding on both parties.

In Masonic Temple Association v. Stockholders Auxiliary Corp., 130 Cal. App. 234, 19 Pac. 2d 865 (1933), the Lodge rented part of its building to a corporation which was authorized to make changes of the premises to serve its purpose. The lease also provided that at the end of the term the premises were to be restored to their original condition. The tenant did not restore the premises at the end of the term, however, the Lodge did and filed suit to recover the amount of money spent to have the work done. The court held that the Lodge could recover the amount spent.

In Masonic Building Association v. Gordon, 88 Kans. 266, 128 Pac. 394 (1912), when a Masonic building was erected it encroached on the adjoining lot and when discovered a sum of money was paid to settle the matter of the encroachment. Suit was later filed claiming that there was still a balance of money due under the agreement. On the basis of the evidence presented the court held that the balance was due from the Lodge.

In Masonic Temple Association v. Harris, 79 Me. 250, 9 Atl 737 (1887), suit was filed to restrain the defendant from obstructing a sewer draining the Masonic Temple which contained stores and offices in addition to Lodge halls. The injunction was issued by the court.

In Masonic Temple Association v. Banks, 94 Va. 695, 27 S. E. 490 (1897), the Masonic Temple was presented with a water accumulation in its basement because the defendant had obstructed the natural flow of water in a creek by erecting a dam. The court entered an injunction against the defendant.

In the Masonic Temple Association v. Channel, 43 Minn. 353, 45 N. W. 716 (1890), the court held that a person who subscribed to buy stock in a building corporation had to pay the amount of the subscription.

But, in Masonic Temple Association v. Kistner, 11 N. J. Misc. 761, 168 Atl. 43 (1933), when suit was filed to collect on a subscription to buy stock to erect a building, with the amount payable in installments, the court held that only the last installment could be recovered because all prior installments were beyond the period of the statute of limitations.

2.9 Property Right Cases.

There are instances where disputes have arisen relative to the rights in property between the Grand Lodge and the constituent Lodges as well as between various Masonic organizations. Here are some illustrative cases.

In Vicksburg Lodge v. Grand Lodge, 116 Miss. 214, 76 So. 572 (1917), the charter of a Lodge was forfeited by the Grand Lodge and a suit was filed to secure the property of the Lodge. The court held that since the Lodge had a corporation charter from the state, it was an entity separate from the Grand Lodge and the property belonged to the corporation and not the Grand Lodge. The facts in this case were unusual because in most instances the Lodge does not have a charter from the state but from the Grand Lodge and the rules of the Craft provide that on dissolution of a Lodge the property reverts to the Grand Lodge.

In Ross v. Sutter, 223 S. W. 273 (1920; Tex. Civ. App.), a Lodge went out of existence without disposing of its property and the property was later sold by the Grand Lodge. A law suit was filed questioning the sale and the court held that it would take judicial notice that the Lodge was no longer in existence and upheld the sale.

In Franklin v. Parallel Lodge, 196 Ark 756, 119 S. W. 2d 1033 (1938), the Grand Lodge law provided that if a Lodge went out of existence its property would go to the Grand Lodge. The Lodge went out of existence in 1930 and its charter was forfeited in 1932. The court held that the Grand Lodge law was against public policy as it amounted to confiscation of property without judicial process, and, therefore, the Grand Lodge had no right to the property.

In Plemenik v. Prickett, 97 N. J. Eq. 340, 127 Atl. 342 (1925), suit was filed by a Lodge to order the Grand Lodge to restore its charter. The charter had been revoked because the Lodge refused to work in the English language as provided by a Grand Lodge rule. The court said on page 342 to 343 "It would be an outrageous thing if the framing of the policies of Masonry could be usurped by this court, because from that it would be but a step to usurping the same power with other like organizations, to the end that property rights would be jeopardized."

A later case was filed entitled United States Savings Bank of Newark v. Schiller Lodge, 117 N. J. Eq. 460, 176 Atl. 330 (1935), in which ten former members of the Lodge claimed money in the bank in the name of the Lodge. The court held that when the charter was revoked its property became the property of the Grand Lodge.

In Franklin v. Burhans, 40 Misc. 566, 82 N. Y. S. 882 (1903), a member, who had charges pending against him while two indictments were pending in which he was the defendant, sought an injunction on the ground that he would be prejudiced in the criminal trial if he was compelled to try the Masonic case first. And that this would amount to taking away from him certain property rights without process of law. The court held on page 883 "A member of the Masonic fraternity has no right in the property of the organization, except that, while a member in good standing, he may enjoy the use of the same in a manner prescribed by the organization."

In Smith v. Smith, 3 Dess. 559 (1817; S. C.), the officers of the "Modern" Grand Lodge and of the "Ancient" Grand Lodge met, settled differences, and decided to unite by forming another Grand Lodge as a "voluntary association". In implementing the settlement certain disagreements arose and suit was filed by the new group to secure the funds of one of the original groups. The court, in a long and detailed opinion, considered the Landmarks of the Craft, and other authorities, and concluded on the basis of state law, that the plaintiff could not recover because the original organization was still in existence, and that the new group was not entitled to the funds.

In Duke v. Fuller, 9 N. H. 536 (1838), a Lodge had been dissolved (apparently as a result of the Morgan affair) and this suit was filed to secure the property of the Lodge. The court held on page 540 "The association may be dissolved, but the trust fund is not therefore, to be either distributed or abandoned. It is an established maxim of equity, that no trust shall fail for want of a proper trustee. The fund of this, and any other charitable institution, may therefore, be saved to carry out the original purposes and wishes of the donors or contributors".

2.10 Provisions in Will.

There are a large number of reported cases involving the validity and the interpretation of wills in which a Masonic group was involved. Here are some illustrative cases.

In Milligan v. Greenville College, 156 Tenn. 495, 2 S. W. 2d 90 (1928), the court held that the intention of the testator in providing in his will that assets be given to the Grand Lodge for the benefit of the Widow's and Orphan's Home could not be defeated because of a misnomer which could be explained by oral testimony.

In Fairview Lodge v. Gladdis, 296 Ill. 570, 130 N. E. 315 (1921), the will left the residuary estate to a Masonic Lodge under certain conditions. After a consideration of the evidence the court held that the conditions prescribed in the will had been met substantially.

In Upham's Will, 289 N. Y. S. 518 (1936), the will provided that equal shares be given to Lodges in two towns in Massachusetts and used for charitable purposes. The Lodges had no legal existence as entities, so the court permitted oral evidence to be introduced and concluded that the legacy be given to the Grand Lodge. The basis of the decision was that a charitable bequest will not be defeated because of a misnomer or indefinite description of the legatee.

In Mason v. Perry, 22 R. I. 475, 48 Atl. 671 (1901), the will of the decedent left money to a Lodge with the provision that it be re-invested until it reached the sum of $50,000, or had increased twenty-five per cent, at which time the income was to be used for charitable purposes, the general expenses of the Lodge, and for occasional entertainment. The court held the bequest void because it ties up the fund indefinitely for purposes other than charity.

In State v. Toney, 141 Ore. 406, 17 P. 2d 1105 (1933), the court held that funds given a Grand Lodge for its home endowment fund could not be diverted by the Grand Lodge to its educational fund. The court followed the well established rule that as long as there are objects that can use the funds as designated, the money cannot be diverted to some other use.

A will gave certain land to the testator's two daughters and their children. A dispute arose and a judgment was entered with all living persons being made parties to the suit. Some forty years later the Masonic Home was about to buy the land and the question arose as to whether the then living grandchildren had any interest in the land. The court held in Masonic Widow's and Orphan's Home v. Hieatt Brothers, 197 Ky. 301, 247 S. W. 34 (1923), that the grandchildren were bound by the former judgment under the doctrine of "virtual representation", which is, that the grandchildren were theoretically parties to the old proceeding and were therefore bound by the judgment.

In Roberts v. Corson, 79 N. H. 215, 107 Atl. 625 (1919), the court held that a devise to a Masonic Lodge "to be used by it as it shall determine best in each case for the benefit of its members who may be in want or distress" created a charitable trust.

In Ingraham v. Sutherland, 89 Ark. 596, 117 S. W. 748 (1909), the will provided that, at the death of the testator's wife and son, the assets be used to build a church and "a Masonic Hall." The court held that the provision was too indefinite and was therefore void.

In Crim v. Williamson, 180 Ala. 179, 60 So. 293 (1912), the court held invalid a bequest to trustees for specified Masonic charities, then added, "but my trustees . . . are not restricted to such charities, but shall exercise wise discretion in aiding worthy objects of charities." The court held the bequest was void for uncertainty.

In Kaufman v. Foster, 3 Cal. App. 741, 86 Pac. 1118 (1906), the court found the Lodge to be formed for charitable purposes and that a trustee appointed by the Lodge to accept and to administer the fund was qualified to receive the money.

In Everett v. Carr, 59 Me. 325 (1871), the court held valid a legacy to a Masonic Lodge which existed as a corporation.

In Cruse v. Axtell, 50 Ind. 49 (1875), a Mason in his will left certain property to his Lodge. Certain of his heirs objected that the Lodge was not organized as the type of entity eligible to take under a will. The court held that the Lodge could take under the will even though the Lodge was not a legal entity because the law favors charitable bequests.

In Hiram Lodge v. Cox, 207 Cal. 106, 277 Pac. 118 (1929), a California resident, in his will, left his estate to an Ohio Lodge and to an Indiana Lodge. The trial court refused to hear evidence that the Lodges were charities on the ground that he was taking judicial notice that they were charitable. But, on appeal the court reversed the decision and remanded the case to the trial court to hear the evidence and then decide.

In Vander Volgen v. Yates, 9 N. Y. 219 (1853), the court held a Masonic Lodge could take real estate under a will given in trust for a charitable purpose.

In Estate of Wiley, 128 Cal. 1, 60 Pac. 471 (1900), the court held that a bequest of property to Masonic bodies "for the use of the widows' and orphans' fund" of those bodies was for a charitable use, and that the court will not assume that the fund will be used for any other purpose expressly declared by the testator.

In Estate of Brown, 140 Cal. App. 2d 677, 295 Pac. 2d 566 (1956), the court held that the Shriner's Hospital for Crippled Children of Colorado, which operates the hospital in San Francisco, and duly authorized to do business in California, can receive a bequest.

In re Heard's Estate, 308 Pac. 2d 502 (Cal. Appl, 1957), the court held that a person making a will would be presumed to know what the law provides and that the term "legal issue" used in a will does not include the adopted child of an heir of the decedent, and therefore, the Masonic Lodge mentioned in the will could share in the assets of the estate. The will left the property to her son and if she died without legal issue the assets were to be given to several persons plus the Grand Lodge and a Masonic Lodge. This decision was vacated in 49 Cal. 2d, 319 Pac. 637.

In re Estate of Fredericks, 311 So. 2d 376 (fla. Ct. of App., 1975), the will provided that all assets be given to his wife and if she died before him then to the Shriners' Hospital. The parties were later divorced, but the will was not changed before his death. The son claimed the estate but the court held that the intention of the decedent, as shown by the will, would prevail and that the divorce in effect made her civilly dead. Under such circumstances his assets went to the hospital.

The courts have adopted a rule that is known as the Cy Pres Doctrine. This has been defined in 14 C. J. S. 512 (1980), as follows: "Cy pres means 'as near to', and this doctrine is one of construction, the reason or basis thereof being to permit the main purpose of the donor of a charitable trust to be carried out as nearly as my be where it cannot be done to the letter". (See also Words and Phrases, Vol. 10A, pp. 558-578).

In Creech v. Scottish Rite Hospital for Crippled Children, 211 Ga, 84 S. E. 2d 563 (1954), the cy pres doctrine was applied. The will made a bequest to the "Masonic Hospital of Georgia for Tubercular Children", which did not actually exist under this name. The doctrine was used to defeat an attack on the gift to a non-existing entity.

In American Bible Society v. Price, 115 Ill. 623 (1886), the court held that eccentricities or peculiarity of views or opinions on religions, colleges, education, Masonry and secret societies will not necessarily render a person incapable of making a will.

In the case entitled In Re Rathbone's Estate, 170 Misc. 1030, 11 N. Y. S. 2d 506, affd. 287 N. Y. 708, 39 N. E. 930 (1942), the will gave assets to a number of Masonic organizations some of which were outside the state where the will was being probated. Each association was considered separately. The bequest to the Shrine Temple was held void became it was not a legal entity. The bequests to the Commandery and to the Scottish Rite failed because they were not charitable or religious organizations. But the bequest to the Masonic Home of Pennsylvania was held valid as a charity.

In the case entitled In re Baldwin, 74 Misc. 325, 134 N. Y. S. 405 (1911), the court held valid a provision in a will making a gift to an unincorporated fraternal association for the purpose of assisting destitute Masons, their widows, and children.

In the case entitled In re Borden's Estate, 142 Misc. 44, 254 N. Y. S. 697 (1931), the bequest of the residue in an estate to a Masonic corporation, in trust to establish and maintain a home for Masons was valid as a completed gift.

In Allaun v. First & Merchant's Bank of Richmond, 190 Va. 104, 56 S. E. 2d 83 (1949), the court held valid a bequest to the Masonic Home in Richmond for 125 years, with the income to be divided annually between six charities at the end of that period.

In Continental Illinois Bank v. Art Institute, 409 Ill. 481, 100 N. E. 2d 625 (1951), the will created a trust which was amended several times. There was mention of the Shriners' Crippled Childrens' Hospital, but the language was ambiguous and the court heard oral testimony on the matter. The court held the hospital not entitled to share in the assets of the estate.

2.11 Power to Exclude Membership in Other Groups.

Frequently the question is asked whether a Grand Body has the authority to provide that its members cannot also be members of another specified group. Usually such a prohibition is made because the other group is considered irregular or its basic principles are not compatible with the principles of Freemasonry. On the basis that associations have the right to determine the qualifications of their members and also the conditions under which membership can continue, such restrictive membership rules have been sustained as being valid. It must be noted that this rule is interpreted to say: You are not being told which other organizations you may join, but if you join such other association you cannot be a member of this association.

Here are the cases relating to the Craft which have considered this question and have applied this general rule:

In Lawson v. Hewell, 118 Cal. 613 (1897), a Royal Arch Chapter had a rule prohibiting its members from belonging to another named group, and the penalty for violating the rule was expulsion. Charges were filed against a member who had violated the rule and a suit was filed to prevent trial on the charges. The court said on page 618:

> Individuals who associate themselves in a voluntary fraternal association may prescribe conditions upon which membership in the association may be acquired, or upon which it may continue, and also prescribe rules of conduct for themselves during their membership, with penalties for their violation, and the tribunal and mode in which the offenses shall be determined and the penalty enforced.

The court also said on page 620:

> Whether it is for the best interests of the order that its members shall not belong to any other orders than those named in the resolutions adopted by the Grand Chapter, or whether membership in the Ancient and Accepted Scottish Rite of the United States jurisdiction is contrary to the best interests of Royal Arch Masonry, are questions pertaining solely to the internal economy of the order, and are purely of Masonic cognizance. Courts have no standard by which to determine the propriety of the rule, and are not competent to exercise any function in the matter.

In Commonwealth v. O'Donnel, 188 Pa. 14 (1898), the By-Laws of a Royal Arch Chapter provided that if a member was suspended or expelled from his Mark Master Mason's group he would ipso factor be suspended from his Royal Arch Chapter. The court held that the restriction was valid.

In Bayliss v. Grand Lodge, 131 La. 579, 59 So. 996 (1912), the court said on page 605 and 606:

> It is clear that, as between itself and its constituents (the Blue Lodges and the membership thereof), the Grand Lodge was within its rights in enacting the law to which we have referred, for the Grand Lodge is a legislative body, created by, and of, those constituents, and the law in question was made by them, through their representatives, to be applied to themselves. It was competent for them, in that way and to that extent, to ordain that, as to their organization, any other body claiming to affiliate or fraternize with them, and particularly one introduction into which requires in some measure, the use of their signs, words, or symbols, is bogus, spurious, and clandestine. . . .

Since this case involved the irregularity of a Cerneau Scottish Rite group, the ruling of this court supports the general Masonic law that each Grand Lodge has the authority to determine what other Grand Lodges or other groups it will consider as "regular" and engage in a relationship with them.

In Eastern Star v. Klutch, 144 Md. 491, 125 Atl. 72 (1924), the Grand Chapter of the Order of the Eastern Star adopted a resolution that prohibited its members from joining the Order of the White Shrine of Jerusalem. In commenting on this rule the court said on page 495:

> The internal policy of the order in regard to the qualifications for membership shall not be questioned by this court, unless some principle is contravened by the provision now being considered.

The court also said on page 495:

> Under the settled law in Maryland we ought not to interfere with the action of the Grand Chapter in deciding a question which was clearly within the legitimate scope of its jurisdiction. As a member of the Eastern Star, the appellee was bound by the agreement embodied in its constitution that the Grand Chapter should determine such a question as the one submitted for its decision, and which she now seeks to have adjudicated in this suit. The judgment of the tribunal

created by the laws of the order should be regarded as final and conclusive in the absence of any suggestion that the right of the appellee to a fair and regular hearing was not duly protected.

An analogous situation existed in England in connection with an association which was not Masonic. In Yeates v. Roberts, 7 De G. M. & G. 227, 3 W. R. 461, affd. 3 Drew 170, 1 Jurs. (n.s.) 319, there was involved an Odd Fellow group in which the rules provided that the group was to be composed exclusively of members of the "Loyal Orange Institution of England". The rules also provided for expulsion of a member who ceased being a member of the Loyal Orange Institution of England. The member involved in this case was expelled and was so notified of his expulsion for that reason. He filed a suit asking that the court order his re-instatement and the court held that he was not entitled to be re-instated as a member.

2.12 Liability for Damages.

Liability for damages for and against associations, their members, and third parties may arise from a variety of situations and are governed by general rules of law. Here are some illustrative cases.

In Thomas v. Dunne, 131 Colo. 20, 279 Pac. 2d 427 (1955), suit was filed against certain individuals and the Al Kaly Temple, of the Shrine, claiming injuries sustained during a ceremony in which the plaintiff received an electric shock while seated on a bench. A verdict was rendered against the Temple, but the court did not impose liability on the individuals.

In Masonic Temple Association v. Collins, 110 Ill. App. 504, 210 Ill. 482, 71 N. E. 396 (1904), a passenger in an elevator, located in the new Masonic Temple in Chicago, was killed when he was caught between the floors of an ascending elevator. A verdict in favor of his family was sustained.

In Masonic Hospital Association v. Taggart, 171 Okl. 563, 43 Pac. 2d 142 (1935), the suit was for damages resulting when a patient in a hospital was given an injection in the arm instead of another part of the body as prescribed by the doctor. The case is of interest only because this happened in a Masonic hospital.

In a non-Masonic case entitled Grand Temple & Tabernacle of Knights and Daughters of Tabor or the International Order of Twelve v. Johnson, 135 S. W. 173 (Tex, Civ. App., 1911), the court held that the Grand Body was not liable for the injuries sustained when harm was done by someone doing something not a part of the ritualistic work. The inference was that the Grand Lodge might have been held liable if the injuries had been sustained while the ritualistic work prescribed by the Grand Body had been complied with. But, this is a highly debatable aspect of the case.

An unusually interesting case which was not appealed is Garlock v. Grand Lodge of the District of Columbia (case number CA 3038-50), filed around the year 1952. The plaintiff was an engineer employed by the Patent Office in Washington. He contended that he had been requested to join a Masonic Lodge and that he refused to do so. He went on to say that the top officers of the Masonic Order controlled the Patent Office and that he was told that if he did not join he would be fired, and that when he continued his refusal he was fired from his job. He filed suit against the Grand Lodge and several members of the Craft for $100,000.00. Several judges of the court were Masons and disqualified themselves from hearing the case. It was then assigned to a judge who was a Roman Catholic.

At the trial it was developed that he had been discharged from his job because he had refused to report for a medical examination as directed by the Patent Office and that his separation from his employment was initiated solely by the Patent Office for this reason and not because of any other person or persons.

During the trial Masons who had served in several high offices of the Craft testified as witnesses. They testified that there is nothing in the rules of Freemasonry requiring its members to discriminate against or to be prejudiced against non-Masons. The plaintiff, who was acting as his own lawyer, on cross examination asked one witness to repeat the Masonic Obligation, and the objection of the attorney for the Grand Lodge was overruled. The witness answered that he had already stated there was nothing in Freemasonry that required its members to be prejudiced against non-members. The judge reconsidered his ruling and then sustained the objection, and the witness was not required to repeat the Obligation.

For cases relating to liability for slander, see Sec. 5.9 below. For a discussion of liability for injuries sustained during initiation see 36 Am. Juris. 2d 395.

2.13 There is no Personal Liability for Opposing ones Membership or for Opposing the Issuance of a Charter.

There are instances where members of the Craft, for reasons best known to themselves, oppose the admittance of one or more persons as members, or oppose the issuance of a charter to a group of members. This may have the effect of preventing these persons from associating with other persons. In such a situation the question may arise whether such conduct will create liability for damages. This question was squarely presented in the case of Trautwein v. Harbourt, 40 N. J. Super. 247, 123 Atl. 2d 30, 59 A. L. R. 2d 1274 (1956).

The facts in the case are briefly stated as follows: Fifty-eight members of the Order of the Eastern Star petitioned the Grand Chapter for a Charter to form a new Chapter of the Order. There was heated and strong opposition to the issuance of the charter and the Grand Chapter decided not to issue it. Suit was filed against the seven persons who actively opposed the issuance of the Charter. The formal printed opinion of the court is long, well reasoned, and each aspect of the case is carefully discussed. The court held there was no liability. The following significant language is used by the court in its opinion:

> Fraternal association implies a degree of social intimacy but one step removed from that of the family. So long as this form of social organization remains as deeply embedded in our culture as it is now, the law must respect it and its ordinary concomitants, chiefly among which is selectivity of membership. Clearly to be implied from the absolutism over admission residing in the organization as an entity is the derivative right of individual members to be heard within the organization on their objections to an applicant and to persuade other members towards their views. To qualify that right by the peril of liability for punitive damages at the suit of an excluded applicant who can convince a jury that the objecting member was motivated by ill will, spite, or prejudice, would be in our judgment, substantially to impair commonly accepted concepts as to freedom of selectivity in social and fraternal organizations, and perhaps, in the long run, to foment and exacerbate rather than relieve the kinds of social stresses which lie beneath the present controversy. There is here apparent a clear 'counter-policy' to the general policy of redressing the intentional inflicting of harm. Cf Ranier's Daries v. Raritan Valley Farms, Inc., 19 NJ 552, 564, 117 A2d 889 (1955). Past unsavory experiences of a member with an applicant may be at once the source of ill will motivating the activity against admission and also a thoroughly justifiable reason for such activity. Other motives may be less justifiable but hardly capable of reliable segregation from good ones by a jury. We do not yet live in the age of the literal brotherhood of man. The 'blackball' continues to hold its place in our frater-

nal life. While courts may be expected continually to tug in the direction of higher ethic, yet, absent legislation, they will wisely wait for new standards of conduct to be invested 'in the minds of the multitude with the sanction of moral obligation' before they invest them with the sanction of the law.

III. MASONIC MEMBERSHIP CASES

3.1 Admission as a Member is a Privilege.

The rule is well established that membership in an association is not a matter of right but is a privilege, and that the group has the absolute right to determine the qualifications and the rules governing the admission of members. (7 C. J. S. 56; 6 Am. Juris. 2d 433; 10 C. J. S. 287; 27 C. J. 899; 36 Am. Juris. 2d 848). In recent years this rule has been relaxed in situations such as labor unions, professional societies, and other groups involving the earning of a living. In 7 C. J. S. 56 (1980), it is stated "A decision of an organization to exclude a person may be arbitrary". But it is also stated that "the standards set for admission into an association, where economic necessity requires membership, must be reasonable, applied evenhandedly, and not be in conflict with public policy".

In Trautwein v. Harbourt, 40 N. J. Super. 247, 123 Atl. 2d 30 (1956), the court said on page 37 "a court will not compel the admission of a person to membership in such an organization who has not been elected according to its rules and by-laws. . . . The general rule is that there is no legal remedy for exclusion of such an individual from admission into a voluntary association, no matter how arbitrary or unjust the exclusion."

3.2 Constitutional Right to Select Associates.

The right of associations to prescribe their own rules relating to the persons it will accept as members is based on the fundamental right of all persons to select the persons with whom they will associate. Therefore, a brief consideration of this constitutional right is in order.

There were a number of cases where the United States Supreme Court intimated that there was a constitutional right to select one's associates. But it was not until it decided National Association for the Advancement of Colored People v. Alabama, 357 U. S. 449 (1959), that the right was stated clearly when the court said on page 460:

> It is beyond debate that freedom to engage in association for the advancement of beliefs and ideas is an inseparable aspect of the 'liberty' assured by the Due Process Clause of the Fourteenth Amendment, which embraces freedom of speech . . . Of course, it is immaterial whether the beliefs sought to be advanced by association pertain to political, economic, religious, or cultural matters.

This right, of course, does have some reasonable limitations. For example, it was held in New York ex rel Bryant v. Zimmerman, 278 U. S. 63 (1928), that reasonable regulation of associations is valid. The enactment of the Civil Rights Act has effected this basic right insofar as some human relationships are concerned. A distinction has been made, and rightfully so, between public contacts and social contacts between persons. Here are some indications in the cases of how fundamental is the private right of association.

In Bell v. Maryland, 378 U. S. 226 (1963), Mr. Justice Goldberg said on page 312:

> Prejudice and bigotry in any form is regrettable, but it is the constitutional right of every person to close his home or club to any person or to choose his social intimates and business partners solely on the basis of personal prejudices including race. These and other rights pertaining to privacy and private association are themselves constitutionally protected liberties.

In Runyon v. McCrary, 427 U. S. 160 (1975), where the court was considering whether a private school was compelled to accept all students irrespective of race, the court made it clear that the cases under consideration (page 167), "do not present any question of the right of a private social organization to limit its membership on racial or any other ground."

In Moose Lodge v. Irvis, Mr. Justice Douglas, in a dissenting opinion, said on page 179 to 180:

> My view of the First Amendment and the related guarantees of the Bill of Rights is that they create a zone of privacy which precludes government from interfering with private clubs or groups. The associational rights which our system honors permit all white, all black, all brown, and all yellow clubs to be formed. They also permit all Catholic, all Jewish, or all agnostic clubs to be established. Government may not tell a man or woman who his associates must be. The individual can be as selective as he desires. So the fact that the Moose Lodge allows only Caucasians to join or come as guests is constitutionally irrelevant as the decisions of the Black Muslims to admit to their service only members of their race.

The Civil Rights Act of 1964 excludes from its application "private clubs" (section 201e). This was intended to preserve the right of persons to select their associates in private and social relationships. What is a "private club" has been the subject of many court cases as persons have tried to evade the application of the Act. (See an extensive annotation on this subject in 8 ALR Fed. 634-669; and 14 C. J. S. Supple. 44).

In this connection Wright v. Salisbury Club, 479 Fed. Supp. 378 (1979), should be consulted because it lists and discusses the various tests which have been used by the courts to determine what is a "private club" under the statute. The decision, however, was reversed in 632 F. 2d 309 (1980), on the ground that the Club had no selectivity in its membership policy, actively solicited members with public advertising, and the Club served the interest of the developer of the Club.

There would be no question that the Craft would fall under the classification as a Private Club under the Civil Rights Act.

Closely related to this subject is the right of privacy which has been recognized in Griswold v. Connecticut, 381 U. S. 479 (1965), and Mapp v. Ohio, 367 U. S. 643 (1960).

On June 26, 1984, the United States Supreme Court decided the case entitled Roberts vs. United States Jaycees. The Jaycees, a group sometimes described as a Junior Chamber of Commerce, restricted its membership to males only between the ages of 18 and 35. Several local Chapters in Minnesota violated this rule and admitted females as members. When the national organization threatened to revoke the Charters of these Chapters a complaint was filed with the Department of Human Rights claiming discrimination under the terms of the state statute. The organization defended the complaint on the ground that the right to select one's associates is a constitutional right and that it did not violate the state statute.

This is a vital legal question. In 1986, for example, a service organization in one of the eastern states was presented with this problem and the court held that women could not be barred from membership.

The language of the court in the Roberts case, making certain distinctions on the application of the general rule, is important and may have relevancy in the future. It is as follows:

> Our decisions have referred to constitutionally protected "freedom of association" in two distinct senses. In one line of decisions, the Court has concluded that choices to enter into and maintain certain intimate human relationships must be secured against undue intrusion by the State because of the role of such relationships in safeguarding the individual freedom that is central to our constitutional scheme. In this respect, freedom of association receives protection as a

fundamental element of personal liberty. In another set of decisions, the Court has recognized a right to associate for the purpose of engaging in those activities protected by the First Amendment-speech, assembly, petition for the redress of grievances, and the exercise of religion. The Constitution guarantees freedom of association of this kind as an indispensable means of preserving other individual liberties.

The intrinsic and instrumental features of constitutionally protected association may, of course, coincide. In particular, when the State interferes with individuals' selection of those with whom they wish to join in a common endeavor, freedom of association in both of its forms may be implicated. The Jaycees contend that this is such a case. Still, the nature and degree of constitutional protection afforded freedom of association may vary depending on the extent to which one or the other aspect of the constitutionally protected liberty is at stake in a given case. We therefore find it useful to consider separately the effect of applying the Minnesota statute to the Jaycees on what could be called its members' freedom of intimate association and their freedom of expressive association.

The Court has long recognized that, because the Bill of Rights is designed to secure individual liberty, it must afford the formation and preservation of certain kinds of highly personal relationships a substantial measure of sanctuary from unjustified interference by the State.

Without precisely identifying every consideration that may underlie this type of constitutional protection, we have noted that certain kinds of personal bonds have played a critical role in the culture and traditions of the Nation by cultivating and transmitting shared ideals and beliefs; they thereby foster diversity and act as critical buffers between the individual and the power of the State. Moreover, the constitutional shelter afforded such relationships reflects the realization that individuals draw much of their emotional enrichment from close ties with others. Protecting these relationships from unwarranted state interference therefore safeguards the ability independently to define one's identity that is central to any concept of liberty.

The personal affiliations that exemplify these considerations, and that therefore suggest some relevant limitations on the relationships that might be entitled to this sort of constitutional protection, are those that attend the creation and sustenance of a family-marriage, e. g., Zablocki v. Redhail, supra; childbirth, e. f., Carey v. Population Services Int'l, supra; the raising and education of children, e. g., Smith v. Organization of Foster Families, supra; and cohabitation with one's relatives, e. g., Moore v. City of East Cleveland, supra. Family relationships, by their nature, involve deep attachments and commitments to the necessarily few other individuals with whom one shares not only a special community of thoughts, experiences, and beliefs but also distinctively personal aspects of one's life. Among other things, therefore, they are distinguished by such attributes as relative smallness, a high degree of selectivity in decisions to begin and maintain the affiliation, and seclusion from others in critical aspects of the relationship. As a general matter, only relationships with these sorts of qualities are likely to reflect the considerations that have led to an understanding of freedom of association as an intrinsic element of personal liberty. Conversely, an association lacking these qualities-such as a large business enterprise-seems remote from the concerns giving rise to this constitutional protection. Accordingly, the Constitution undoubtedly imposes constraints on the State's power to control the selection of one's spouse that would not apply to regulations affecting the choice of one's fellow employees. Compare Loving v. Virginia, 388 U. S. 1, 12 (1967) with Railway Mail Ass'n v. Corsi, 326 U. S. 88, 93-94 (1945).

Between these poles, of course, lies a broad range of human relationships that may make greater or lesser claims to constitutional protection from particular incursions by the State. Determining the limits of state authority over an individual's freedom to enter into a particular association therefore unavoidably entails a careful assessment of where that relationship's objective characteristics locate it on a spectrum from the most intimate to the most attenuated of personal attachments. See generally Runyon v. McCrary, 427 U. S. 160, 187-189 (1976) (POWELL, J., concurring). We need not mark the potentially significant points on this terrain with any precision. We note only that factors that may be relevant include size, purpose, policies, selectivity, congeniality, and other characteristics that in a particular case may be pertinent. In this case, however, several features of the Jaycees clearly place the organization outside of the category of relationships worthy of this kind of constitutional protection.

The undisputed facts reveal that the local chapters of the Jaycees are large and basically unselective groups. At the time of the state administrative hearing, the Minneapolis chapter had approximately 430 members, while the St. Paul chapter had about 400. Report A-99, A-100. apart from age and sex, neither the national organization nor the local chapters employs any criteria for judging applicants for membership, and new members are routinely recruited and admitted with no inquiry into their backgrounds. See I Tr. of State Administrative Hearing 124-132, 135-136, 174-176. In fact, a local officer testified that he could recall no instance in which an applicant had been denied membership on any basis other than age or sex. Id., at 135. Cf. Tillman v. Wheaton-Haven Recreational Ass'n, 410 U. S. 431, 438 (1973) (organization whose only selection criteria is race has "no plan or purpose of exclusiveness" that might make it a private club exempt from federal civil rights statute); Sullivan v. Little Hunting Park, Inc., 396 U. S. 229, 236 (1969) (same); Daniel v. Paul, 395 U. S. 298, 302 (1969) (same). Furthermore, despite their inability to vote, hold office, or receive certain awards, women affiliated with the Jaycees attend various meetings, participate in selected projects, and engage in many of the organization's social functions. See Tr. 58. Indeed, numerous non-members of both genders regularly participate in a substantial portion of activities central to the decision of many members to associate with one another, including many of the organization's various community programs, awards ceremonies, and recruitment meetings. See, e. g., 305 N. W. 2d, at 772; Report A102, A103.

In short, the local chapters of the Jaycees are neither small nor selective. Moreover, much of the activity central to the formation and maintenance of the association involves the participation of strangers to that relationship. Accordingly, we conclude that the Jaycees chapters lack the distinctive characteristics that might afford constitutional protection to the decision of its members to exclude women. We turn therefore to consider the extent to which application of the Minnesota statute to compel the Jaycees to accept women infringes the group's freedom of expressive association.

3.3 Jurisdiction.

The word "jurisdiction" has many meanings but as used here it means the power to hear a specific matter. The word in court covers two broad areas, jurisdiction over the person and jurisdiction over the subject matter. In the context used here the subject must, by necessity, be exceedingly brief. Anyone interested in the subject is referred to classic Masonic texts for a discussion of the subject insofar as it applies within the Craft, and to general law books insofar as it applies to the courts.

One area that has presented a problem is the well stated rule that if a member of the Craft is charged with a Masonic offense and he lives outside the state where he holds his Masonic membership, he can be tried either where he resides or where his Lodge is located. Coil's Masonic Encyclopedia, page 336; Mackey, Jurisprudence of Freemasonry, page 388 to 389; 1927 ed.; Henry M. Look, Masonic Trials, page 27; 1902; John W. Simons, a Familiar Treatise on the Principles and Practices of Masonic Jurisprudence, page 84 to 86; 1864). In the 1949 Proceedings of the Grand Lodge of Illinois, the Grand Master reported that a member residing outside the state had been charged with unmasonic conduct involving moral turpitude and had been expelled after a trial before a trial commission. He then stated, "Illinois has always respected such action as was taken by this lodge in another Grand Jurisdiction; accordingly, I issued an order accepting the action of the lodge in this case, notified the man's own lodge of his expulsion and ordered that his name be stricken from the roll of membership." There is no question that this statement of Masonic law would be sustained by the courts at this time because it is in accord with established general rules of law.

The old common law rule was announced in the famous case of Pennoyer v. Neff, 95 U. S. 714 (1877), where the court held that a state had no authority to enter a personal judgment against a non-resident not served with a summons within the state where the court is in session. But in Milliken v. Meyer, 311 U. S. 457 (1940), the court held that a state retained its power over its citizens even when they reside outside the state; the ground for the decision was that the state had power over its citizens residing outside the state because absence does not dissolve the duties and responsibilities of citizenship, therefore, a summons can be served on a citizen in another state and a valid personal judgment could be entered against him. The relationship between a Lodge and a member residing outside the jurisdiction of the Lodge would be analogous.

In International Shoe Co. v. Washington, 326 U. S. 310 (1945), the court held that a non-resident corporation who did business in a state thereby made itself subject to its jurisdiction and could be sued in the courts of that state. This general rule over the years has been expanded in a large number of cases and has been applied to a variety of situations. These decisions are a necessary development from the ease with which persons move freely from place to place in their personal and business relationships. Under the rules of the Craft, and also under general rules of law, a non-resident Mason can be tried for a Masonic offense in his own Lodge or in the Lodge of the place where he resides at the time. In the normal course of events when two tribunals have concurrent jurisdiction the charges are usually filed in the place where the offense took place because of the availability of the evidence there as well as the convenience in trying the matter. Once the decision is rendered, the question arises whether the result is binding on the Lodges in other states and particularly on the Lodge where the persons hold his Masonic membership. Here again resorting to the general rules of law is helpful.

The United States Constitution (Art. IV, Sec. 1) provides, "Full Faith and Credit shall be given in each State to the public Acts, Records, and judicial Proceedings of every other State." This provision establishes the general policy of recognizing official acts that have taken place outside the state. There is also established what may be described as the "rule of comity" which is well stated in Somportex Limited v. Philadelphia Gum Corporation, 453 Fed 2d 434 (1971), where the court was presented with the question whether a judgment rendered by a court in England should be recognized and enforced in this country. The court held that the judgment should be recognized and enforced using the following language on page 440:

> Comity is a recognition which one nation extends within its own territory to the legislative, or judicial acts of another. It is not a rule of law, but one of practice, convenience, and expediency. Although more than mere courtesy and accommodation, comity does not achieve the force of an imperative or obligation. Rather, it is a nation's expression of understanding which demonstrates due regard both of international duty and convenience and to the rights of persons protected by its own laws. Comity should be withheld only when its acceptance would be contrary or prejudicial to the interest of the nation called upon to give it effect.

This language, by analogy, would apply to the situation we have been considering.

3.4 Termination of Membership.

The constitution and by-laws of an association constitute a contract between the group and its members and are binding on both unless they are immoral, contrary to public policy, or the law of the land (6 Am. Juris. 2d 435). Under this general rule an association has the power to establish general rules pertaining to suspending or expelling a member (7 C. J. S. 59; 1980). It has been held that a member may be expelled for violating a law of the association even if the rule is unreasonable (7 C. J. S. 60; 1980). The courts are reluctant to interfere in the internal affairs of an association and ordinarily will not review the expulsion of a member from an association, but, the rule is otherwise where the membership is a matter of economic necessity or is necessary for the practice of a profession (7 C. J. S. 58; 1980).

There are situations where membership in an association may be terminated without notice to the member (36 Am. Juris. 2d 854). These are usually situations where the facts are not in dispute, are easy to ascertain, and the rules of the association so provide. An illustration is when dues have not been paid. But the general rule is that where punishment is sought against a member he is entitled to notice of a hearing and be given an opportunity to be heard (6 Am. Juris. 2d 463). Here are some illustrative cases relating to Freemasonry.

In accordance with the general rule, membership in a Masonic group cannot be terminated without notice and an opportunity to be heard. (Universal Lodge v. Valentine, 134 Md. 505, 107 Atl. 531, 1919 and Evans v. Brown, 134 Md. 519, 107 Atl. 335, 1919).

It has been held that a court cannot interfere with the internal affairs of an association unless property rights are involved, general rules of law are being violated, or the rules of the group have been violated as illustrated in the cases which follow.

In Rogers v. Tangiers Temple, 112 Neb. 166, 198 N. W. 873 (1924), a group of Shriners formed a club and campaigned for the election of officers by circulating sample ballots and using indecent language about the Potentate. This was in violation of the rules of the Shrine and the Imperial Council suspended these members. A suit was filed to enjoin the Shrine Temple from excluding them from the affairs of the Shrine and the court held it had no power to consider the matter.

In Hershiser v. Williams, 11 Ohio Dec. 76 (1895), the court observed that a Masonic Lodge is an organization not for profit, has power to expel a member and determine what is un-Masonic conduct. A court of equity has no authority to try a member for expulsion since no property rights of the member are involved even though the Lodge is proceeding irregularly.

In Franklin v. Burnham, 82 N. Y. S. 882 (1903), suit was filed by a member to stop a Masonic trial on the ground that a criminal case was pending against him for having committed a criminal libel. And to defend himself in the Masonic trial would prejudice him in the criminal case because he had to disclose his defense. The court held it had no power to stop the Masonic trial.

In Ellerbe v. Faust, 119 Mo. 653, 25 S. W. 390 (1894), the Grand Lodge had adopted a resolution that saloon keepers could not be members. Faust was a saloon keeper and resigned his membership. He was also a member of a Masonic Benefit Association which followed the lead of the Grand Lodge and amended its rules to bar saloon keepers. But Faust continued to pay his assessments. Later the association became insolvent and levied a special assessment and when Faust did not pay this assessment a suit was filed against him. The court held that Faust was not liable.

In Connelly v. Masonic Mutual Benefit Association, 58 Conn. 552 (1890), a member had been suspended, but after his death as a result of an investigation it was determined that he had not been properly notified since the summons was not in proper form as provided by the Grand Lodge rules. The order of suspension was revoked and he was re-instated to membership. The court held that the widow was entitled to receive on the benefit certificate even though the re-instatement occurred after the death of the member.

An unusual case was Robinson v. Yates City Lodge, 86 Ill. 598 (1877). The plaintiff had been a member of the Lodge and was expelled. He sued for the return of his degree fees and the court applied the general rules of contract law and decided he was not entitled to recover.

In Rutledge v. Gulian et al, 93 N. J. 113 (1983), a Grand Master had sponsored a travel tour for the members of lodges in his state. The travel agency that handled the matter sent him a commission check of $18,800 which the Grand Master kept. After his term of office this payment was discovered and he refused to give the money to charities as his two predecessors had done. He contended that this money was paid to him for work performed and also because he had not gone on the tour for free as was customary in such matters for the promoter. Suit was filed against him and the court held he could not keep the money. Charges were then filed against him even though he paid over the money and he was suspended from membership in the Craft. He filed suit to have this order vacated and the court held against him. Later disciplinary proceedings were filed against him before the Supreme Court of the state since he was a lawyer and it was contended, on the above facts, that he was guilty of unprofessional conduct. In the case entitled Matter of Rutledge, 101 N. J. 493 (1986), the court held that he acted improperly and he was reprimanded. Although he has endeavored on numerous occasions to be reinstated in his Lodge, to date his request has not been granted.

3.5 Procedure in Termination Cases.

As a general rule, a member cannot be suspended from or expelled from an association without a fair trial before an impartial tribunal (7 C. J. S. 63). And a reasonable opportunity must be given to defend the charges filed (Evans v. Brown, 134 Md 519, 107 Atl. 535, 1919 and M. W. Grand Lodge v. Lee, 128 Md. 42, 96 Atl. 872, 1916). It is established that the proceedings to discipline a member should be conducted in conformity with the rules of the association and the law of the land (7 C. J. S. 61, 1980). Here are some illustrative cases.

In Masonic Grand Chapter of the Order of the Eastern Star v. Sweatt, 29 S. W. 2d 334 (1959), a member engaged in conduct that disrupted a Grand Chapter meeting, and she disobeyed the presiding officer. By order of the Grand Chapter she was expelled from the Order. The rules of the Order provided that on the death of a member certain insurance benefits were payable to her named beneficiaries. The court stated on page 447, "If appellee's punishment had been limited to the deprivation of the fellowship in which membership entitled her, a different question would have been presented. Deprivation of pecuniary benefits resulting from contractual relations is a different proposition, and is governed by different principles of law. The former may not involve dues process, but the latter does." The court held she was entitled to be heard because of the pecuniary rights involved.

In Robinson v. Yates City Lodge, 86 Ill. 598 (1877), charges were filed against a Lodge member and he was notified of the date set for the hearing on the matter. The member notified the Master of the Lodge that he would be unable to attend the hearing because the date interfered with his duties as County Surveyor and the hearing was held in his absence. The court held that merely telling the Master that he was unable to attend did not deprive the Lodge of the power to proceed to hear the matter.

In Everson v. Order of the Eastern Star, 265 N. Y. 112, 191 N. E. 854 (1934), the court held that a member of a fraternal organization cannot be charged with one offense and then be found guilty of another offense.

3.6 Courts Have Limited Powers in Termination of Membership Cases.

The courts in various situations have adopted the rule that its power in the internal affairs of private associations is limited.

THE COURTS AND FREEMASONRY

The general rule is that courts will not interfere with the action of an association in suspending or expelling a member, although it may do so when such action was wrongful. Ordinarily a suspended or expelled member should exhaust his remedies within the association before appealing to the courts for relief (7 C. J. S. 65, 1980 and 6 Am Juris. 2d 453, 472). The decision of the tribunal of an association with respect to its internal affairs will be accepted by the courts in the absence of mistake, fraud, illegality, collusion, or arbitrariness (6 Am. Juris. 2d 454). A court will not retry a case heard before the tribunal of the association. It will only inquire if the rules of the association have been complied with, the proceeding was in good faith, and whether there has been any violation of the law of the land (6 Am. Juris. 2d 466).

In Connelly v. Masonic Mutual Benefit Association, 58 Conn. 552 (1890), the court said on page 556:

> . . . the Masonic organization has a due and orderly system of laws and rules, enacted by itself and enforced by its own agencies, in accordance with which membership in any lodge is acquired, continued, or lost; and that all questions of membership or nonmembership, or of good standing in any lodge, or of any affiliation or nonaffiliation, are by these laws and rules within the jurisdiction of their own officers, and that when any such question has been passed upon by their own tribunals, subordinate and appellant, the decision is conclusive and binding upon all Masons.

In Franklin v. Burhan, 40 Misc. 566, 82 N. Y. S. 884 (1903), the court said on page 884:

> It is the province of all courts constituting the civil judiciary to take cognizance only of those rights which flow from the common law, legislative enactments, political constitutions, and international treaties. The right of membership in the Masonic fraternity springs from no one of those sources. Membership therein confers no legal right of which a court of equity will take cognizance . . . The Masonic fraternity is an unicorporated society, which has customs and laws of its own. The plaintiff voluntarily became a member thereof, and in so doing submitted himself to the customs and laws of the organization, and for any alleged infraction of those customs and laws by the plaintiff it is his duty to stand trial in the forum constituted by the organization, and at the time and in the manner prescribed.

In Lawson v. Hewell, 118 Cal. 613 (1897), the court said on page 619:

> In all matters of policy, or of the internal economy of the organization, the rules by which the members have agreed to be governed constitute the charter of their rights, and courts will decline to take cognizance of any matter arising under these rules. Whether the rules have been violated, or whether members have been guilty of conduct which authorizes an investigation by the association or the imposition of the penalty prescribed by it, is eminently for the association itself to determine, and, if the investigation is in accordance with the rules, the party charged has no ground of complaint, since it is but carrying into effect the agreement he made when he became a member of the association.

In Most Worshipful Grand Lodge v. Grimshaw, 34 Dist. of Col. App. 383 (1910), a group of black men withdrew as members of a Lodge calling itself "Masonic" and formed a new Lodge. For ten years both groups functioned at the same time. The name of one of the groups had the word "Ancient" in it. This suit was filed to stop one of the groups from functioning. The court held it had no authority to decide which of the two groups was the genuine organization.

In Mead v. Stirling, 62 Conn. 586 (1892), in discussing a Masonic tribunal the court said on page 597, "The general principle is that a court of chancery is not the proper tribunal to correct the errors and irregularities of inferior tribunals, and that in ordinary cases the court would not interfere." It was claimed that the persons who were to act as judges were not in fact qualified to act.

In Grand Chapter v. McRobinson, 147 La. 63, 84 So. 495 (1920), the plaintiff sought an injunction against the defendant who was claiming she was the Grand Matron whereas she was not so elected. It was alleged that the acts of the defendant were causing confusion, bringing discredit to the group, and will irreparably injure the plaintiff. The injunction was refused. The decision was approved on appeal because no pecuniary interest was involved in the matter.

In Kopp v. White, 65 N. Y. S. 1017 (1900), the court said on page 1019:

> The privilege of membership in an unincorporated, voluntary, association, like the one under consideration, is not given by statute or derived from prescription, as in a corpora-

tion, but is created and conferred by the organization itself, and may be withheld or conferred at the pleasure of the association, and under such rules and restrictions of the association as it may see fit to establish. . . . Individuals who form themselves into a voluntary association for a common object may agree to be governed by such rules as they think proper to adopt, if there is nothing in them in conflict with the law of the land.

In Smith v. Merriott, 130 Md 447, 100 Atl. 731 (1917), the court held it had no power to stop a trial about to be held in a Grand Body. The member being tried contended that the officers making a demand for funds in his possession were not properly elected. The court held it had no power to determine the validity of the election.

3.7 Right of Members to Property of the Group.

Generally speaking, if a member abandons or leaves an association he thereby renounces or loses whatever interest he may have in the assets of the association, and the members who remain succeed to his interest (6 Am. Juris. 2d 450; 7 C. J. S. 70, 1980). Here are some illustrative cases.

In Duke v. Fuller, 9 N. H. 536 (1838), the Lodge, having been reduced to eight members, one of them sued the treasurer for his proportion of the Lodge funds. The court held that the member did not have a severable interest in the Lodge funds and that the money had been collected for and were to be used for Masonic purposes.

In Hamilton v. White, 42 Ariz. 170, 22 Pac. 2d 1089 (1933), many members had left an Eastern Star Chapter. These members then secured a Charter from the Grand Chapter of Texas and sued for the funds in the original Chapter. The court held that the funds belonged to the original Chapter.

In Curien v. Santini, 16 La. Ann 27 (1861), a Lodge had fifty members of which forty-two voted to withdraw from the Grand Lodge and eight dissented. The seceders filed suit to secure the assets of the original Lodge. The court held that the new Lodge was not entitled to the funds on the ground that a Lodge cannot be dissolved even against the will of the minority.

In Rogers v. Tangier Temple, 112 Neb. 166, 198 N. W. 873 (1924), the court held that it had the power to inquire whether proceedings to expel the plaintiffs had been held in conformity with the rules of the Shrine and to protect property rights. It then went on to hold that the members of a Shrine Temple had no individual personal rights in the assets of the Temple.

In United States Savings Bank v. Schiller Lodge, 117 N. J. Eq. 460, 176 Atl 330 (1935), the majority of a Lodge's members had left the Lodge and joined another Lodge. The Grand Lodge rule stated that the funds of a dissolved Lodge belonged to the Grand Lodge. The court held that the assets of the dissolved Lodge did not belong to the members, but to the Grand Lodge, as provided by the law of the organization.

In Smith v. Smith, 3 Dess. 559 (S. C., 1817), the court held that where a new Lodge is formed by members withdrawing from the former Lodge it is not entitled to the funds of the first group. The court, in a long and detailed opinion, considered the Landmarks of the Craft and the well established rules of law generally which provide that the members of a new organization have no standing in court so long as the original association is in existence.

In Phillips v. Widow's Son Lodge, 152 Va. 526, 147 S. E. 193 (1929), a majority of the members present at a meeting voted to withdraw from the Grand Lodge and then took over the property of the Lodge. The court held that this could not be done since there were members able to function as the old Lodge.

In Gross Lodge v. Brausch, 256 Ill. 186, 99 N. E. 9087 (1912), a non-Masonic organization, which operated under the Grand Lodge system, has a provision in its rules stating that if a constituent Lodge ceased to exist all its assets became the property of the Grand Lodge. The court held that this provision was valid. It also held that the members of a constituent Lodge, even by unanimous vote, divide the funds among themselves or transfer them to another Lodge.

IV. TAXATION AND FREEMASONRY

There has been a lack of uniformity in the court cases involving the subject of taxation relating to Freemasonry. The main reason for this situation is that there are always state constitutional provisions, as well as statutes, involved in such cases and these provisions are never the same in every place. This is especially true in the cases involving the taxation of real estate owned and used by Masonic organizations. For this reason such questions as arise on this subject must be considered on all occasions on an individual basis in the light of the then existing local law. Here we will present the cases in each state briefly for your guidance only and as leads to the existing cases. There is no assurance that your local courts will follow any specific case decided in another state, or even those decided in your state, especially if the statute has been changed in the meantime.

It is also noted that the decision of a court as to the tax status of real estate for a specific year is not binding in later years (Oak Park Club v. Brenza, County Collector, 7 Ill. 2d 389, 131 N. E. 2d 89, 1956 and Grand Lodge v. Burlington, 84 Vt. 202, 78 Atl. 973, 1911).

4.1 Real Estate Tax Cases.

Alabama

In Ware Lodge v. Harper, 236 Ala. 334, 132 So. 59 (1938), the court held that the Act of Incorporation which created the formal establishment of the Craft as an entity in the state exempted Masonic property from taxation. This was held to be a contract and therefore could not be changed by an Act of the legislature.

Arizona

In Conrad v. Maricopa County, 40 Ariz. 390, 12 Pac. 2d 613 (1932), the court held that the statute exempting all "charitable institutions" did not exempt Masonic property. The court took the view that tax exemption statutes are strictly construed against the exemption, and therefore the word "institution" did not include "property".

Arkansas

In Grand Lodge v. Taylor, 146 Ark. 316, 226 S. W. 129 (1920), the court held that the law exempting "buildings and grounds and materials used exclusively for public charity" did not exempt the property of a Masonic Lodge. The court stressed the point that the property was not being used "exclusively" for the purpose stated in the statute.

Colorado

In Horton v. Colorado Springs Society, 63 Colo. 529, 173 Pac. 61 (1918), the court held that under the constitutional provision exempting property used solely and exclusively for charitable purposes a Masonic Temple was exempt from taxation.

In Commissioners v. San Luis Valley Masonic Association, 80 Colo. 183, 250 Pac. 147 (1926), the court held exempt from taxation a park owned in trust for the Masonic Fraternity and used by Masons for summer recreation.

In Elm Jebel Shrine Association v. McGlone, 93 Colo. 334, 26 Pac. 2d 108 (1933), the Shrine bought a lot and erected a foundation on it with the intention of later constructing a building on it to serve the benevolent and charitable purposes of the Shrine. The statute exempted a lot with a building constructed on it for use as a charity. The court held that the property was exempt and that it was not necessary to have a complete structure on the lot to come within the exemption.

In Creel v. Pueblo Masonic Building, 100 Colo. 281, 68 P. 2d 23 (1937), the building was owned by a purely charitable association but parts of the building were used for commercial purposes by tenants. The funds received were used to pay the expenses of operating the building and the balance for purposes of the Association. The court held that the rented parts of the building were not incidental to the main purposes of the organization, and therefore the real estate was not exempt from taxation.

In City of Denver v. George Washington Lodge Association, 121 Colo. 470, 217 Pac. 2d 617 (1950), the court held not exempt from taxation a vacant lot owned by a Masonic association on the ground that it was not being "used" for charitable purposes.

Connecticut

In Masonic Building Corporation v. Town of Stamford, 119 Conn. 53, 174 Atl. 301 (1934), a building was used sixty-five per cent for Masonic purposes and the balance as an auditorium, kitchen, bowling alley, billiard room, etc. from which a small income was received. The court held that the property was not exempt because it was not being used as a school, for public worship, or exclusively for charitable purposes.

Florida

In State ex rel Gragor Co. v. Jones, 150Fla. 486, 8 So. 2d 15 (1942), the court held that the use of the property, and not the nature of the ownership, is the determining factor in deciding whether the property is exempt. The court held the property not subject to taxation.

In Simpson v. Bohon, 159 Fla. 280, 31 So. 2d 406 (1947), the court held that the portion of a building owned by a Masonic association that is used for commercial purposes is taxable.

In Rogers v. City of Leesburg, 157 Fla. 784, 27 So. 2d 70 (1946), the court held that a Lodge building belonging to the trustees of a fraternal association was exempt from taxation though a part of the building was rented to tenants.

Georgia

In The Mayor of Savannah v. Solomon's Lodge, 53 GA. 93 (1874), the court held that a Masonic Lodge is a charitable institution and its property is exempt from taxation.

In Massenburg v. Grand Lodge, 81 Ga. 212, 7 S. E. 636 (1888), the court held that the portion of a building owned by a Masonic organization which was rented for stores was not exempt from taxation even though the income was devoted to charitable purposes.

In Atlanta Masonic Temple v. City of Atlanta, 162 Ga. 244, 133 S. E. 244 (1926), the court held that the property of a Masonic organization was not exempt from taxation merely because its income was devoted to a charitable purpose.

Illinois

In Grand Lodge v. Board of Review, 281 Ill. 480, 117 N. E. 1016 (1927), the court held exempt from taxation the farm used to house and maintain old and destitute Masons and their widows.

In The People v. Freeport Masonic Temple, 347 Ill. 180, 179 N. E. 672 (1931), the court held exempt from taxation the Scottish Rite Cathedral in Freeport, but, this decision was expressly overruled later in 359 Ill. 593, 596.

In The People v. Dixon Masonic Temple Building Association, 348 Ill. 593, 181 N. E. 434 (1932), the court held that a Masonic Temple was not exempt from taxation.

In The People v. Rockford Masonic Association, 348 Ill. 567, 181 N. E. 428 (1932), the court held that a Masonic Temple is not exempt from taxation because the primary purpose of the occupancy was not charitable.

Cook County Masonic Temple Association v. The Department of Revenue, 104 Ill. App. 3rd 658; petition for leave to appeal denied, 91 Ill. 2d 58 (1982). On the basis of the evidence presented the court held that Masonic Temples were used primarily for charitable purposes and that the other uses were incidental to this primary purpose. Therefore, the Temples were exempt from real estate taxes.

Indiana

In City of Indianapolis v. The Grand Master, 25 Ind. 518 (1865), the statute exempted "every building erected for the use of any benevolent or charitable institution." The structure in question was owned and used by Masonic organizations and was used partly by commercial establishments. The court held that the property was not exempt from taxation though some of the income was devoted to charitable purposes.

In State Board of Tax Commissioners v. Trustees of Adoniram Lodge of Perfection, 250 N. E. 2d 605 (1969), the court held that real estate of the Scottish Rite used for the furtherance of educational, religious, and fraternal purposes was exempt from taxation.

In Sahara Grotto v. State Board, 261 N. E. 2d 873 (1970), the court held that the real estate owned and operated by the Grotto was not exempt from taxation.

See "Opinions of the Attorney General of Indiana," 1900-1902, page 118 and 262.

Iowa

In Lacy v. Davis, 112 Iowa 106, 83 N. W. 784 (1900), the court held that property owned by the Knights Templar and used for meetings and as a summer retreat for the members was not exempt from taxation.

In Morrow v. Smith Wilson's Estate, 145 Iowa 514, 124 N. W. 316 (1910), the court held a Masonic Lodge was a charitable institution, engaged in no business for profit, its income being used for Lodge expenses and the remainder for charity, the real estate was exempt from taxation.

The Attorney General of the state in 1934 rendered an opinion that Masonic Lodges occupying a building does not exempt the structure from taxation even though the total receipts from the rented portion of the property is devoted to charitable and benevolent purposes.

Kansas

In Mason v. Zimmerman, 81 Kans. 799, 106 Pac. 1005 (1910), the court held that the property owned and used by the Grand Lodge was not exempt from taxation. The statute exempted "all property used exclusively for . . . benevolent and charitable purposes".

In Masonic Home v. Sedgwick County, 81 Kans. 859, 296 Pac. 734 (1910), the court held exempt from taxation real estate used for the care and nursing of old persons who were members of the Eastern Star.

In Mahattan Masonic Temple Association v. Rhodes, 132 Kans. 646, 296 Pac. 734 (1931), the court held a Masonic Temple was not exempt from taxation.

In Clement v. Ljungdahl, 161 Kans. 274, 167 Pac. 2d 603 (1946), the court held that a building used exclusively by Masonic organizations and owned by five of them was not exempt from Taxation.

Kentucky

In Commonwealth v. Masonic Temple, 87 Ky. 349, 8 S. W. 821 (1888) and 89 Ky 658, 8 S. W. 699, the court held that a Masonic Temple was not exempt from taxation.

Masonic Temple Co. v. Commonwealth, 11 Ky L. R. 383, 12 S. W. 143 (1899), an appeal was dismissed on technical grounds.

Masonic Temple Co. v. Planz, 21 Ky. L. R. 583, 52 S. W. 821 (1899), interpreted the statutes relative to action forgiving payment of real estate taxes and then held that the statute of limitations did not run while case was pending.

In City of Newport v. Masonic Temple Association, 108 Ky. 333, 56 S. W. 405 (1900), the law exempted the property of institutions of "purely public charity". The court held that the property of a Masonic Lodge was not exempt.

In Vogt v. City of Louisville, 173 Ky. 119, 190 S. W. 695 (1917), the court held that a home maintained by the Knights Templar was not tax exempt because it was not an institution of purely public charity.

Louisiana

In State ex rel Bertel v. Board of Assessors, 34 La. Ann. 574 (1882), the court held that Masonic organizations are charitable institutions and their property is exempt from taxation, but that the property involved in this case, owned by the Scottish Rite and rented out in part for stores was not exempt.

In Grand Lodge of Masons v. New Orleans, 44 La. Ann 659 (1892), the court held that a statute exempting Masonic property could be changed as it did not constitute a contract, since it was a mere gratuity. This decision was affirmed in 166 U. S. 143 (1897).

In Bangor v. Masonic Lodge, 73 Me. 428 (1882), the court held that the property used for stores and Masonic halls was not exempt from taxation as it did not come within the term "benevolent, charitable and scientific."

Maryland

In Appeal Tax Court v. Grand Lodge, 50 Md. 421 (1878), the Grand Lodge owned a building in which there were stores on the first floor. The court held that an exemption statute does not constitute a contract and can be changed at a later date; that property is exempt while used for a charitable purpose if it is used partly not for profit that portion of the building is not exempt.

In Mayor v. Grand Lodge, 60 Md. 280 (1883), the court held that those parts of a building owned by a Masonic organization that are used for commercial purposes are not exempt from taxation.

Massachusetts

In Masonic Education & Charity Fund v. Boston, 201 Mass. 320, 87 N. E. 602 (1909), the court held that the funds being accumulated by a Masonic organization for the purpose of establishing a Home for indigent and needy Masons was not exempt from taxation.

In Worcester Masonic Charity and Educational Association v. Assessors, 326 Mass. 409, 94 N. E. 2d 763 (1950), the statute exempted real estate "owned and occupied by . . . benevolent, charitable and scientific institutions". The court held the property in question was not exempt from taxation because it was not proved that the ownership and the occupancy was by the association.

Michigan

In Attorney General v. Detroit Common Council, 113 Mich. 388, 71 N. W. 632 (1897), the court held that a Masonic Temple owned by an association was not exempt from taxation. The court took the position that exemption exists when the association owns the property and directly engages in the activity described in the statute.

Mississippi

In Senter v. City of Tupelo, 136 Miss. 269, 101 So. 372 (1924), the court held the particular building was not exempt from taxation. The statute exempted property uses for "fraternal and benevolent purposes," but this particular property was rented to others and the income was used to pay the mortgage.

Missouri

In The State v. Central St. Louis Masonic Hall Association, 14 Mo. App. 596 (1884), the court held that property purchased for the purpose of erecting a Masonic Temple was not exempt from taxation.

In Fitterer v. Crawford, 157 Mo. 51, 57 S. W. 532 (1900), the court held that the portion of the building used for Masonic purposes was exempt from taxation but that the part rented to others was not exempt though the income was used for charitable purposes. The court observed that there is a difference between using the property for charitable purposes and using the rents for that purpose.

Nebraska

In Plattsmouth Lodge v. Cass County, 79 Neb. 463, 113 N. W. 167 (1907), the court held exempt property not used exclusively by a Masonic Lodge.

In Mt. Moriah Lodge v. Otoe County, 101 Neb. 274, 162 N. W. 639 (1917), the court held that the facts in the record failed to show the real estate was exempt from taxation because the amount used for charity was minor and too indefinite.

In Scottish Rite Building v. Lancaster County, 106 Neb. 95, 182 N. W. 574 (1921), the court held that a building owned by the Scottish Rite was not exempt from taxation because it was not used "exclusively" for religious and charitable purposes.

In Ancient and Accepted Scottish Rite v. Board, 122 Neb. 586, 241 N. W. 93 (1932), the court held that property of the Scottish Rite was not exempt from taxation.

In Masonic Temple Craft v. Board of Equalization, 125 Neb. 841, 252 N. W. 313 (1934), under the law of the state the holder of a mortgage on real estate is considered having a taxable interest in the real estate; this also reduces the value of the taxable interest of the owner of the real estate. The decision was modified in 129 Neb. 293, 261 N. W. 569 (1935).

In McDonald v. Masonic Temple Craft, 133 Neb. 589 and 135 Neb. 48 (1938), the court held that property used partly for Lodge purposes and partly for commercial purposes was entirely exempt from taxation on the ground that the court had no authority to determine what part was taxable.

New Jersey

In City of Trenton v. Trenton Masonic Temple Association, 8 N. J. Misc. 778, 151 Atl. 753 (1930), affd. 108 N. J. L. 419, 158 Atl. 395 (1932), a number of Masonic organizations owned a building that was used exclusively for Masonic purposes. The court held that the property was not exempt from taxation. The court observed, if any of the bodies had been the owner of the building, the property would have been exempt.

In Alpine Masonic Temple Association v. State Board of Tax Appeals, 15 N. J. Misc. 275, 190 Atl. 782 (1933), the court held that a Masonic Temple was not exempt from taxation.

New Mexico

In Temple Lodge v. Tierney, 37 N. Mex. 179 (1933), the court held that the property used by various Masonic organizations but owned in trust was exempt from taxation.

New York

In People ex rel Syracuse Masonic Temple v. Ostrander, 105 Misc. 405, 173 N. Y. S. 356 (1918), the court held that a Masonic Temple was exempt from taxation.

In People ex rel Buffalo Consistory v. Betz, 114 Misc. 124, 185 N. Y. S. 538 (1921), the court held property not exempt from taxation because part of the building was rented to tenants.

In People v. Breder, 121 Misc. 553, 201 N. Y. S. 291 (1923), a building was owned by a corporation but was used by various Masonic groups. The court held that the property was not exempt from taxation because it was not proved that the entire net income from the building was used for charitable purposes.

In People ex rel Troy Masonic Hall v. Byrne, 125 Misc. 312, 210 N. Y. S. 527 (1925), the court held real estate used for fraternal purposes was not exempt from taxation.

In The People v. Clark, 125 Misc. 625, 210 N. Y. S. 360 (1925), the building was used by various Masonic organizations. The surplus money of the Lodges was used to maintain a Masonic Home. More than half the building was used for recreation and entertainment. The court held that the property was not exempt from taxation because it was not used "exclusively" for that purpose.

In People v. White, 218 Misc. 38, 217 N. Y. S. 657 (1926), the court held property owned by a Masonic hall association was not exempt from taxation.

In People v. Farrell, 130 Misc. 142, 223 N. Y. S. 660 (1927), the court held exempt from taxation property used as a Masonic Home.

In Plattsburg Lodge v. Laravie, 127 Misc. 275, 238 N. Y. S. 327 (1929), the court held the property was not exempt from taxation because it was not used "exclusively" for the purposes set forth in the statute.

In People v. Goldfoyle, 136 Misc. 100, 241 N. Y. S. 328 (1929), the court held that property of a Masonic temple association was not exempt from taxation because the use of the property, rather than the use of the funds for charitable purposes, is the test.

In the Matter of Syracuse Masonic Temple, 224 App. Div. 38, affd. 270 N. Y. 8 (1936), the court held the property was not exempt because the evidence did not disclose that the net proceeds were devoted to the purpose set forth in the statute.

In People v. Miller, 164 Misc. 726, 1 N. Y. S. 2d 1267 (1937), affd. 279 N. Y. 137, 18 N. E. 2d 8 (1938), the court held that a Masonic Temple was exempt from taxation though some of the income from the real estate was used to maintain a Masonic Home in another part of the state.

In German Masonic Temple Association of the City of New York v. City of New York, 279 N. Y. 452 (1939), the court held the property involved not exempt from taxation because the owner collected rent from the occupants even though the income was devoted to the maintenance of charitable Homes.

In Ithaca Masonic Temple v. Calistri, 57 Misc. 2d 72, 291 N. Y. S. 2d 721 (1968), the court held the property not exempt from taxation.

North Carolina

It is likely that the courts would hold Masonic property not exempt because of the case entitled Sir Walter Lodge of Odd Fellows v. Swain, 217 N. C. 632, 9 S. E. 2d 365 (1940). In deciding this case the court cited the following case in support of its ruling, Grand Lodge v. Taylor, 146 Ark. 316, 226 S. W. 129 (1920), a Masonic case.

North Dakota

In State v. Packard, 35 N. D. 298, 160 N. W. 150 (1916), the court held exempt from taxation real estate used by various Masonic groups.
Ohio

In Application of Cincinnati Masonic Temple, 98 N. E. 2d 244 (1950), the Board of Tax Appeals held that restaurant equipment used by Masons and their friends was not exempt from taxation.

Oklahoma

In State v. Bartlesville Lodge, 168 Okl. 416, 33 Pac. 2d 507 (1934), the statute exempted property of fraternal organizations. The court held that a part of a building used for Masonic purposes was exempt from taxation.

Pennsylvania

In Philadelphia v. Masonic Home of Pennsylvania, 160 Pa. 572, 23 Atl. 954 (1894), the court held that the property was not exempt from taxation because it was not a "public charity" since the benefits were restricted to Masons. (See related case in 33 Pa. Super. 382, 1907).

South Carolina

In State v. Addison, 2 S. C. 499 (1871), the court held that the real estate was not exempt from taxation merely because it was leased to a Lodge.

South Dakota

In Scottish Rite Temple Association v. County, 62 S. D. 204, 252 N. W. 626 (1934), the court held exempt from taxation a building owned by the Scottish Rite and occupied as a residence by its secretary.

Tennessee

In Lodge Cumberland v. Nashville, 127 Tenn 248, 154 S. W. 1141 (1912), the court held the property exempt from taxation on the ground that the Masonic Lodge was engaged in charitable activities and the income of the Lodge helped support the Masonic Home.

Texas

In Morris v. Lone Star Chapter, R. A. M., 68 Tex. 698, 5 S. W. 519 (1887), the court held that the property was not exempt from taxation.

In City of Houston v. Scottish Rite Benevolent Association, 111 Tex. 191, 230 S. W. 978 (1921), and 233 S. W. 551 (1921), the court held that the Scottish Rite Cathedral was not exempt from taxation as it was not used for "purelypublic charity."

In Masonic Temple Association v. Amarillo, 14 S. W. 2d 128 (Tex. Civ. Appl, 1928), the court held that the property involved was not exempt from taxation.

Utah

The statute exempts real estate used "exclusively for either religious worship or charitable purposes."

On the basis of two cases decided relating to the Elks and the Odd Fellows it would appear that real estate of fraternal bodies are not exempt. (Salt Lake Lodge No. 85, Elks v. Groesbeck, 40 Utah 1, 1911 and Odd Fellows' Building v. Naylor, 53 Utah 111, 1918).

Vermont

In Grand Lodge v. Burlington, 84 Vt. 202, 78 Atl. 973 (1911), the real estate was rented to tenants but the proceeds were used for the purpose (as contended) within the statute. The court held that property not exempt from taxation.

In Grand Lodge v. Burlington, 104 Vt. 515, 162 Atl. 368 (1932), the building's first floor was rented for stores, the second in part for offices, with the balance of the building being used for Masonic purposes. After the expenses of operating the building were paid the balance was used for securing a Masonic Home and other charitable uses. The court held the property was not exempt from taxation.

Virginia

The state statute exempts property "used for Lodge purposes or meeting rooms of such associations, together with such additional land as may be necessary for the convenient use of the buildings for such purposes."

In City of Richmond v. Grand Lodge of Virginia, 162 Va. 471, 174 S. E. 846 (1934), the court held that the portion of Masonic property not used for Lodge purpose was subject to taxation.

West Virginia

In Re Masonic Temple Society, 90 W. Va. 441, 111 S. E. 637 (1922), the court held that a building used solely for Masonic Lodge activities was exempt from taxation, though the statute used the word "purely" and the word "exclusively", on the ground that these types of associations should be helped and therefore the statute should be liberally construed in their favor.

In State v. McDowell Lodge, 96 W. Va. 611, 123 S. E. 561 (1924), the real estate was used partly by Masonic organizations and partly for commercial activities. The court held that the use of the property and not the use of the funds determined whether the real estate was exempt from taxation. The specific property involved was held not to be exempt.

Wyoming

In Harding v. Rock Springs Lodge, 23 Wyo. 522, 154 Pac. 323 (1915), the statute exempted "lodge rooms for the meeting of all secret, benevolent and charitable societies". The building involved in this case was a Masonic Temple which was rented occasionally to churches and clubs for various functions. The court held the property was exempt from taxation.

4.2 Inheritance Tax Cases.

In Clarke v. Union Trust Co. of the District of Columbia, 192 Md. 127, 63 Atl. 2d 635 (1949), the court held that the bequest to the Shriners' Hospital for Crippled Children was not exempt from inheritance taxes because it was to a foreign corporation and a substantial part of its charitable work was outside the state.

In Re Estate of Schureman, 8 Ill. 2d 125, 133 N. E. 2d 7 (1956), involved a will which gave part of the assets to a Masonic Temple Association and to a Masonic Board of Controls. The court observed that the gift was not limited to the benevolent and charitable activities of the fraternal associations. It therefore held that the gift was subject to inheritance tax.

In re Wilson's Estate, 145 Iowa 514, 124 N. W. 316 (1910), the court held a devise of real estate to a Masonic Lodge was exempt from inheritance tax.

In Everett v. Carr, 59 Me. 325 (1871), the court held a gift to a Masonic Lodge to be used for the relief of human suffering was exempt from inheritance tax.

In McDonald v. Stubbs, 142 Me. 235, 49 Atl. 2d 765 (1946), the court held that a legacy given in trust for a Masonic Lodge, the income to be used to pay Grand Lodge dues and to maintain the building which was partly rented, was not exempt from inheritance tax.

In Thirkell v. Johnson, 150 Me. 131, 107 Atl. 2d 489 (1954), the court held that a gift to a Masonic Lodge was not exempt from inheritance tax because it was not to a benevolent or charitable institution.

In MacGregor v. Commissioner, 327 Mass. 484, 99 N. E. 468 (1951), a will left funds to a Lodge and to a commandery. The court held that the funds were taxable since the charitable activities were not restricted to Massachusetts but extended beyond the state.

In Old Colony Trust Co. v. Commissioner, 331 Mass. 329, 119 N. E. 2d 175 (1954), the court held a bequest to the Supreme Council Charity Fund was exempt, but a bequest to a Masonic Lodge was not exempt from inheritance tax.

In Estate of Burrough, 357 Mo. 10, 206 S. W. 2d 340 (1947), the court held that to be exempt from inheritance tax the charitable work must be within the state. The court also held that funds given in a will to erect a Masonic Temple for use by three Masonic Lodges was exempt from inheritance tax since this was for a charitable purpose.

In People ex rel Crook v. Wells, 179 N. Y. 257, 71 N. E. 1126 (1904), the court held a gift given in a will was exempt from inheritance tax because the Masonic Guild was a charitable organization.

In re Allen, 70 Misc. 88, 136 N. Y. S. (1912), the court held exempt from inheritance tax a bequest to the Trustees of the Masonic Home and Asylum Fund.

In Re Hiteman, 110 Misc. 617, 180 N. Y. S. 880 (1920), the court held exempt from inheritance tax a bequest to a local Masonic Lodge to erect a Temple and to purchase the site for the building on the grounds that the Lodge was a charitable and benevolent organization.

In Tax Commission v. Security Savings Bank and Trust Co., 117 O. S. 442, 159 N. E. 570 (1927), the court held that a bequest of money to be invested for fifty years and then given to a Masonic Home for Masons and members of their families was not exempt from inheritance tax because it was not used "for the purposes only of public charity."

In Robert's Will 193 Wis. 415, 214 N. W. 347 (1927), the court held that a bequest to a Masonic Lodge was not exempt from inheritance tax because it was not "organized solely for religious, charitable or educational purposes."

In Estate of Silverthorn, 274 Wis. 452, 80 N. W. 2d 430 (1957), the court followed the rule in the preceding case.

In Estate of Thronson, 243 Wis. 73, 9 N. W. 2d 641 (1943), the court held a bequest to a bank exempt from inheritance tax because on the happening of certain contingencies the assets went to the Masonic Home.

4.3 Estate Tax Cases.

In First National Bank of Dallas v. Commissioner of Internal Revenue, 45 Fed. 2d 509 (1930), the court held that a bequest to several appendant Masonic Bodies was taxable as the entities were not corporations and were not organized or operating exclusively for charitable purposes.

In Levey v. Smith, 103 Fed. 2d 643 (1939), the will gave certain assets to a Scottish Rite Body. The Body contended that the assets were to be used exclusively for charitable and educational purposes. The court held the gift taxable, but stated that if the assets were intended to be used for the purpose contended the testator should have so specified.

4.4 Miscellaneous Tax Cases.

In Masonic Aid Association v. Taylor, 2 S. D. 324, 50 N. W. 93 (1891), the association issued death benefit certificates to its members which was restricted to Masons in good standing. The court held that the association was a mutual benefit society and was taxable and not exempt under the statute exempting from taxation fraternal and secret societies.

In Masonic Country Club of Western Michigan v. Holder, 12 Fed. 2d 951 (1926), the statute imposed a tax on the initiation fees of certain clubs but exempted organization under the Lodge system. The court held that the country club involved was not exempt from payment of the tax. But this decision was reversed in 18 Fed. 2d 553 (1927).

In application of Cincinnati Masonic Temple, 94 N. E. 2d 244 (1950), the court held that restaurant equipment in a Masonic Temple was not exempt from taxation.

V. COURT TRIALS

5.1 Parties to Suit.

In every law suit there must be at least two parties. One will be the plaintiff and the other will be the defendant. The plaintiff will be contending that his rights have been infringed upon by the defendant. A party to a law suit must be a person, this means an individual or an entity created or recognized by law, such as a corporation (59 Am. Juris. 2d 333).

Today most Lodges and other groups of Masons are organized as legal entities with the power to sue and to be sued. In the early days, however, this was not always the situation and there are a number of old cases that held that Masonic Lodges could not sue or be sued in their Lodge names as they had no legal existence as a "person" or as an "entity." (Nightingale v. Barney, 4 Greene 106, Iowa, 1853; Brooks v. Owen, 200 Iowa 1151, 202 N. W. 505, 1925 and Cohn v. Borst, 36 Hun, 562, 1885).

The general rule is that in the absence of a statute authorizing it to be done, an unincorporated association (sometimes called a voluntary association) cannot sue as such in the name of the group, but must file suit in the name of the individual members (7 C. J. S. 91, 1980 and 6 Am. Juris. 2d 485). Also, as a general rule such an association cannot be a defendant unless permitted by statute (7 C. J. S. 99, 1980).

There is a conflict of views on whether such associations can be viewed as partnerships or whether they are to be considered as entities and be a party to a suit (36 Am. Juris. 2d 813).

Here are some illustrative cases:

In Nightingale v. Barney, 4 Greene 196 (1853), suit was filed to recover on a note given to a Lodge officer of a Masonic Lodge in payment of initiation fees and the note was then indorsed to the plaintiff who sued for the benefit of the Lodge. The court held on page 106 and 107, "None but a natural person or an artificial person can become a party to a suit. An unincorporated association such as a masonic Lodge, cannot be recognized as a person or party at law, and hence cannot sue or be sued . . ." The court held that the suit could not be maintained because the Lodge was the real party in interest.

In Ionic Lodge v. Masons, 232 N. C. 252, 62 S. E. 2d 73 (1950), the suit was filed by an unincorporated association against a corporation whose charter had been suspended. The court held that the suit could be filed in the name of the association and that the suspension of the charter did not bar the filing of the suit.

In Torrent Lodge No. 711 v. National Surety Co., 231 Ky. 302, 21 S. W. 2d 439 (1929), the court held that a Lodge treasurer had authority to start and maintain a suit in the name of the Lodge. The suit was filed to recover money claimed as a default of the former treasurer of the Lodge.

5.2 Must Exhaust Remedies Within Organization Before Can File Suit.

The general rule is that before a person can seek the help of a court in a dispute with a fraternal organization he must first exhaust all remedies afforded him within the group (36 Am. Juris. 2d 842 and 6 Am. Juris. 2d 456). This means that if the rules of the organization provide for an appeal this procedure must be filed as a condition precedent to filing a court case. But there have been extreme and unusual situations where this rule has been disregarded (6 Am. Juris. 2d 456, 469 and 844). Here are some Masonic cases illustrating the rule.

In Lawson v. Hewell, 118 Cal. 613 (1897), the court said on page 621, "So long as he has this right of redress within the order he has no right to invoke the aid of the courts".

In Mead v. Stirling, 62 Conn. 586 (1892), the court said on page 592 to 593, ". . . the society remedies must be pursued to their very end first, and that ultimate unfairness alone can be remedied by outside tribunals".

In United Grand Lodge v. Lee, 128 Md. 42, 96 Atl. 872 (1916), a member was tried before a trial commission and he was suspended. He contended that certain rules had been violated in filing the proceedings. On appeal the court observed that although the remedies within the association had not been exhausted, since some of the Grand Lodge rules had not been followed the court could proceed to hear the matter.

5.3 Remedies Available.

The remedies sought in cases involving the Craft are the same as in other cases. The claim may be for a breach of contract, or the commission of a tort. The plaintiff may be seeking money damages, a court order commanding that the defendant do something, or an injunction preventing the defendant from doing something. It is always important that the correct remedy be sought in connection with the claimed wrong. For example, in Costa v. Luna Servante, 225 Ala. 6, 49 So. 2d 672 (1950), a member of a mystic society who had been expelled sought an injunction to prevent the association from interfering with her rights as a member because she claimed the expulsion was null and void. The court held that the injunction remedy was not proper but that the plaintiff should pursue the remedy of mandamus which would order the association to expunge the order of expulsion if her contention was correct.

Suits against charitable organizations may present a problem. Claims against them for breach of contract can be maintained (14 C. J. S. 544). But there is no uniformity on whether a charity can be sued in tort as a matter of public policy (14 C. J. S. 544). The reason for this view is that money and property held by a charitable association is held in trust and must be used for the main purpose of the group and cannot be diverted for any other purpose.

In 20 A. L. R. 2d 344, there appears a detailed discussion of the subject "Suspension or Expulsion from Social Club or Similar Society and the Remedies Therefor."

In De Villars v. Hessler, 363 Pa. 498, 70 Atl. 2d 333 (1950), a fraternal organization had a concession at a County Fair. A person was hurt when a steam table exploded. There was no formal organization and the court held that the members were engaged in a joint venture for a charitable purpose and therefore there was no liability.

The general rule is that anyone having a legal right must pursue it promptly, but the courts have not been applying this rule with any degree of uniformity because all the facts and circumstances are always considered and the results are different. Here are some illustrations of how the rule of "laches" [undue delay in asserting a right or privilege] has been applied. In Faisan v. Adair, 144 Ga. 797, 87 S. E. 1080 (1916), the plaintiff was the white Shriner organization and the defendant was the black Shriner organization. An injunction was sought to keep the defendant from imitating the name, regalia, etc., of the white group. Both associations were operating in the same city. The question of laches was raised and the court remanded the case to the trial court. The jury held that the plaintiff was not guilty of laches in the filing of the suit. In Burell v. Michaux, 279 U. S. 737 (1929), with the same situation existing in Texas, the court held the plaintiff was guilty of laches because there was a seventeen year wait before suit was filed.

5.4 Eligibility Of Judge In Masonic Cases.

On a number of occasions the question has been raised whether a judge, who is a member of the Craft, is qualified to preside in a trial which involves a Masonic group or a Mason. The general rule has been stated as follows:

> A judge is not per se disqualified to try a cause, where

> one of the parties to which is a church, lodge, or society of which he is a member. (36 Am. Juris. 2d 174).
>
> The fact that the judge is a member of a church, lodge, society or educational institution may, but does not necessarily, disqualify him from acting in a suit in which the organization is interested, or to which it is a party. (48 C. J. S. 1050).

Here are some illustrative cases where this general rule has been involved where the judge has been a member of the Craft:

In Blackeman v. Harwell, 198 Ga. 165, 31 S. E. 2d 50 (1944), a suit was filed to secure the construction of the terms of a will; the Scottish Rite Hospital for Crippled Children was a party to the suit. The trial judge was a Mason. Five of the Supreme Court Justices were Masons, but none of the Justices belonged to the Scottish Rite. The question was raised as to the qualification of the judges to hear the case. The court on page 172, quoting from 15 R. C. L. 528 said:

> From earliest times it has been held that the requirements of impartiality disqualifies a judge from acting in a case in which he has an interest. Though it has been held that the disqualificating interest may be a personal one to the judge, the general rule is that it must be pecuniary in nature, and not remote, uncertain, speculative or merely incidental; and several cases emphasize the distinction between a property interest and such interest as results from a feeling of sympathy or bias that would disqualify a juror.

And quoting from another work the court said:

> The interest which disqualifies a judge is a direct pecuniary or direct property interest, or some which involves some individual right or privilege in the subject-matter of the litigation, whereby a liability or pecuniary gain must occur on the event of the suit.

In Masonic Building Corporation v. Carlsen, 128 Neb. 108, 258 N. W. 44 (1934), the court held that the trial judge, a Mason, was not disqualified to preside at a trial in which his Lodge owned some shares of stock in a corporation which was one of the parties to the suit. Objection to him to so preside was made near the end of the trial which took eleven days, and his rulings did not appear to be influenced by his Lodge membership.

In Odom v. Langston, 356 Mo. 1140, 205 S. W. 2d 518 (1947), the case involved the construction of the terms of a will in which the Masonic Home of Missouri was one of the beneficiaries. Objection was made that the judges were Masons and therefore not qualified to decide the case. The court held that such membership did not disqualify the trial judge or any of the Supreme Court judges.

In Masonic Fraternity Temple Association v. City of Chicago, 131 Ill. App. 1 (1907), one of the Appellate Court justices assigned to hear the case disqualified himself from taking part on the ground that he was a shareholder of the Temple Association.

5.5 Mason as Juror in Masonic Cases.

The question is sometimes raised whether a Mason is qualified to serve as a juror in a case involving a Masonic group or a fellow member. The general rule is set out in 50 C. J. S. 976 as follows:

> The fact that a person is a member of a particular order, association, or other organization does not, as a general rule, of itself render such person incompetent as a juror.

Here are some illustrative cases:

In Noonan v. Saline County Coal Co., 173 Ill. App. 541 (1912), four prospective jurors were objected to because they were members of a union. The court in its decision on page 544 said:

> Membership in the organization was the only ground of challenge urged, and it has been held that it is not grounds for challenge that a juror and one of the parties are members of the same corporation, association or secret society.

In Sebring v. Weaver, 42 Pa. Super. 588 (1910), the court held that it was not a disqualification to serve as a juror solely on the ground that he was a Mason and one of the parties was a Mason.

In Burdine v. Grand Lodge of Alabama, 37 Ala. 478 (1861), the court held that since a Masonic Lodge is a charitable organization a member of the Lodge can serve as a juror since his pecuniary interest in the outcome of the case is small and remote.

In Purple v. Horton, 13 Wend. 9 N. Y. (1834), objection was made of three prospective jurors on the ground that they were Masons and the plaintiff had been a Mason but had resigned. The court held that the prospective jurors were not disqualified to serve. There is one unusual aspect of the case in that the purported oath is printed in full in the court decision as presented in evidence by one of the witnesses.

In Forrester v. State, 95 Tex. Crim. Rep. 62, 252 S. W. 785 (1923), the prosecuting attorney objected to the attorney for the defendant asking prospective jurors as to their Masonic membership stating that he would not ask if the prospective juror in a trial of a Mason was a Mason. The court held that the remark was not ground for reversal.

In State v. Stonestreet, 112 W. Va. 668, 166 S. E. 378 (1932), the basic question was the hostility between two competing groups calling themselves "Masonic" and each accusing the other of being clandestine. The court held it was proper to ask prospective jurors if they were members of either of the groups. The ground of the ruling was that a party is entitled to know under the circumstances whether the prospective juror was a member of a rival order so that the party could exercise his right of a peremptory challenge of the prospective juror.

Additional cases on this subject can be found in 31 A. L. R. 418 and 158 A. L. R. 1369.

5.6 Final Argument Making Reference To The Craft.

At the end of a jury trial the attorneys usually present a final argument to the jury designed to summarize the case. In a number of instances it has been contended that during said argument statements were made referring to some aspect of the Craft which was made to prejudice the jury. Here are several illustrations.

People v. Bowman, 24 Cal. App. 781, 142 Pac. 495 (1914), was a prosecution for securing the execution of a note under false pretenses. In the final argument the prosecutor stated "I know that he defrauded a brother Mason, done it fraudulently and intentionally". The court held this was an unwarranted statement, but was not reversible error as it did not appear that any of the jurors were Masons.

In Craven v. State, 22 Ala. App. 39, 111 So. 767 (1927), the attorney for the state in his final argument said, "I know that there are some good Masons in this jury and some of you are good Ku Klux Klansmen". The court held that the statement was improper but not sufficiently prejudicial to require a new trial.

In State v. Howard, 120 La. 311, 45 So. 260 (1907), the court held it was proper for the prosecuting attorney in his final argument to the jury to say, "I am sure that this jury will not be influenced by the testimony of this congregation of Negro witnesses that Ben Howard, a big Mason and Church member has been able to procure to prove the innocence of his son, Silas Howard."

5.7 Evidence.

The general rules of evidence are many, technical, and hard to understand because of the many exceptions. These rules, of course, are applicable in cases involving Freemasonry. Here are some illustrative cases.

In Swisher v. Fidelity & Deposit Insurance Co., 164 Ill. App. 243 (1911), the court held that the written records of a Lodge, if available, are the best evidence of its proceedings.

In Leach v. Dodson, 64 Tex. 185 (1885), the court held that the records of a Masonic group were admissible in evidence to show action of the group, and that it was proper to consider records produced by the presiding officer, there being no secretary and the acting secretary being sick.

In Masonic Mutual Benefit Association v. Severson, 71 Conn. 719 (1899), the by-laws of the association were silent as to the change that had been made at a later date. The court held that oral testimony as admissible to prove the change made since the provisions of the by-laws at the time of death of a member, and not the time when the person joined the association, determined who would receive the death benefit.

In Howard v. Russell, 75 Tex. 171, 12 S. W. 525 (1889), a question of pedigree was involved in an estate being probated. Copy of a petition for membership in a Masonic Lodge was offered in evidence as well as a copy of the minutes of the Lodge. The court held these documents were admissible in evidence as ancient documents more than thirty years old. The court stated that the Craft was "an ancient and well-established society".

In Estate of Wirt, 207 Cal. 106, 277 Pac. 118 (1929), the will was being probated in California and left gifts to a Masonic Lodge in Ohio and one in Indiana. The court held it could not take judicial notice of these Lodges being charitable organizations and that proof was necessary because the two groups existed outside the state.

In Territory v. McGrath, 16 N. M. 202, 114 Pac. 364 (1911), a statute made it a misdemeanor to operate a house of prostitution within 700 feet of a benevolent or fraternal society. The defendant was charged with having operated such a house within the prescribed distance and was found guilty. The court on appeal held that it would take judicial notice that a building used by the Masons and the Knights of Columbus were being used by benevolent or fraternal organizations.

In Burdine v. Grand Lodge of Alabama, 37 Ala. 478 (1861), the court held that since a Masonic Lodge is a charitable organization a Mason was qualified to be a witness in a case involving a Masonic Lodge since his financial interest was small. The court also held that a contract was admissible in evidence even though there was a variance between the statute creating the Grand Lodge and the charter issued to a subordinate Lodge in that the words "Most Worshipful" were omitted in the title.

In Continental Illinois National Bank v. Art Institute, 409 Ill. 481 (1951), a suit to construe a trust agreement, the document stated it could be changed at any time and the creator of the trust did make several changes. The court held that it could hear oral testimony to make clear any ambiguous language in the instrument.

In Masonic Mutual Benefit Society v. Strickland, 97 Mo. 137, 10 S. W. 895 (1899), suit was filed on a surety bond, and in considering the testimony of a witness the court said on page 896:

> . . . where the evidence is the result of voluminous facts, or of the inspection of many books and papers, the examination of which cannot conveniently take place in court, or where a witness has inspected the accounts of the parties, though not allowed to give evidence of the particular contents, he will be allowed to speak of the general balance or result of such examination, and such statement is not hearsay.

Questions are sometimes raised whether a person will be permitted to testify in case because of a specific exclusionary rule of evidence. In the administration of justice there is the rule that the court has the right and the duty to hear each man's evidence. But there are situations where the testimony of a witness is excluded for a variety of reasons. For example, at common law an interested person was not qualified to testify unless it was the only evidence available; therefore, shareholders of a corporation were not qualified to testify (81 Am. Juris. 2d 149). But it has also been held that a statute that disqualifies "parties" as witnesses does not exclude shareholders of a corporation since they are a separate entity (81 Am. Juris. 2d 390). A further statement of the rule is set forth in 97 C. J. S. 2d 548, as follows:

> Incompetency might also result from the situation of the witness as a member of, or stockholder in, a corporation or association which was a party, or his position as an officer of such corporation or association, although where the witness could neither benefit nor receive a detriment as a result of the action, he was permitted to testify.

In Masonic Temple Association v. City of Atlanta, 162 Ga. 244 (1926), the court held that it was not admissible to have a witness testify that he had made a study of the Masonic Order and that he had found it to be a charitable organization. The court intimated that the testimony might have been admissible if the witness had been qualified and an expert on the subject.

In State v. Morgan, 145 La. 585, 82 So. 711 (1919), in a prosecution for murder a negro defendant wore a Masonic ring. The prosecuting attorney asked the defendant "Since when did you put on that ring there, and by what authority are you wearing it? Isn't it your intention to escape the gallows by wearing it?" The court held the last question objectionable, but held further that this was not reversible error since the jurors were instructed to disregard the question.

5.8 Libel and Slander Cases.

While in the United States we have a constitutional right of freedom of speech, there is a limitation on this right when words are spoken or written which injure another person. Under certain conditions the words spoken which injure another are considered privileged communications and cannot be the basis for a claim. The general rule relating to this subject is set forth in 53 C. J. S. 194:

> Communications published during the course of proceedings before religious, fraternal, and other like organizations, and representations made by a member of a church, lodge or society regarding the character or conduct of another member or candidate for membership, are protected by a qualified privilege; but such privilege affords no protection if abused.

It has also been stated in 50 Am. Juris. 2d 715, as follows:

> It is generally recognized that a qualified privilege attaches to statements and communications made in connection with the various activities of such organizations as lodges, societies, labor unions, and professional associations. Thus, so long as they act without malice, and not actuated by improper motives, officers and members of such bodies, may, without liability for any resultant defamation, report on the qualifications of applicants, comment on the qualifications and activities of members, prefer charges against members, or officers, offer testimony in support of the charges,

properly publish disciplinary action that may be taken, comment on the qualifications of candidates for office in the organization, communicate with each other as to the preservation of funds and the plaintiff's control as financial secretary, and report on tension with the association and criticize governing officers.

Here are some illustrative cases on the subject.

In State v. Drake, 122 S. C. 350, 115 S. E. 297 (1922), the defendant was indicted for libel. The court permitted in evidence a letter written by the defendant. The court said on page 351:

> Appellant wrote the letter in confidence to the Master of the lodge, after he had been charged with violation of the rules of the order, and threatened with being disciplined by the order, in defense of the charge that had been practically preferred against him. He did not intend that it should go further than the Master and brethren of the lodge; he did not publish the libel, but the Master of the lodge made the contents of the letter public when he received it. It was a privileged communication to the lodge through its Master. It was a confidential letter to his brother Masons, in defense of his good name and standing in the order, and such a letter was confidential and privileged.
>
> The Masonic order has the right to investigate any violations of the rules of the order and to discipline its members if found violating its rules. And any member, in his defense, had the right to defend himself, and to regard his communication to the lodge as privileged and imparted in confidence and secrecy, and not to be made public outside the lodge room to others than members of the order.

In Nix v. Caldwell, 81 Ky. 293 (1883), the plaintiff and the defendant were not Masons. One testified at a Masonic trial and the other signed an affidavit that the plaintiff could not be believed under oath. Suit was filed claiming plaintiff had been slandered. The court held that although the statements made at such a trial usually are privileged communications, when made by non-members of the group, they are not privileged and can be the basis of a claim.

In Turnage v. New Bern Consistory, 215 N. C. 798, 3 S. E. 2d 8 (1939), the court held that a Scottish Rite Body is not immune from a slander action solely because its net profits derived from a moving picture show went to a crippled children's hospital.

In Campbell v. Masonic Chronicler Publishing Co., 214 Ill. App. 601 (1919), suit was filed to recover damages for publishing an article that clandestine promoters were arrested as imposters in advertising for men desiring to become Masons. The court held that the complaint had sufficient allegations to state a cause of action.

In Campbell v. Morris, 224 Ill. App. 569 (1922), the court held that it is not slanderous per se to state that a candidate for public office had demitted from his Lodge and "poses as a Mason in good standing" and that the suit could not be maintained since there was no allegation of fact stating what damages had been sustained by the plaintiff.

In Fisher v. Myers, 339 Mo. 1196, 100 S. W. 2d 551 (1936), a suit for libel was filed resulting in a substantial judgment against certain defendants. The facts stated in the opinion are long and detailed but they disclose that Mrs. Fisher was active in the Order of the Eastern Star and served as Grand Matron of the Order in Missouri. At the annual meeting of 1928 of the Grand Chapter a printed pamphlet was circulated that Mrs. Fisher had engaged in immoral conduct some years before. One defense was that the communication was privileged. The court observed on page 567 that the statements made were not before a tribunal hearing evidence on filed charges or investigating Mrs. Fisher, and, therefore the information was not privileged.

In Berot v. Porte, 144 La. 805, 81 So. 323 (1919), a case not involving Masons, it was held that one who applies for membership in a secret society is charged with notice that his character and reputation will be investigated, and cannot complain of the disclosures made unless he can show actual malice.

5.9 Confidential Communication Between Masons.

Every Mason is morally bound not to repeat any statement made to him in confidence by another Mason. But the question arose in one case whether such an obligation is legally binding in a court proceeding.

In Owen v. Frank, 7 Wyo. 457, 53 Pac. 282 (1898), a witness refused to testify in court on the ground that the matter had been communicated to him in confidence by a brother Mason. The court said on page 462:

> It is perfectly clear that at common law the conversation would not have been privileged. . . .
>
> Neither does the statute include such a conversation among privileged communications. . . .

THE COURTS AND FREEMASONRY

And the court explained its decision by using the following language on page 463:

> However binding an obligation may be, as between members of the same society, secret or otherwise, not to divulge to others that which may be confidentially communicated to them, such an obligation must be understood to be subject to the law of the country, and doubtless the societies themselves recognize that such a limitation attached to an obligation; and therefore it cannot be said that the obligation is violated when the disclosure is compelled in a court of justice, in the course of the administration of the laws.

This case and the subject is discussed by Judge Newell A. Lamb (a Past Grand Master in Indiana), in *Masonic Trials and Privileged Communications*, The Masonic Service Association, 1984.

5.10 Embezzlement Cases.

There have been a few instances where officers of Masonic associations have embezzled funds of the group and the courts have entered into the matter of discipline. Here are some illustrative cases.

In Washbon v. Hixson, 86 Kans. 406, 121 Pac. 518 (1912) and 87 Kans. 310, 124 Pac. 366 (1912), the Grand Treasurer used a Grand Lodge check to pay a personal debt. The court held that the recipient of the check was on notice from the wording on the check that the Grand Lodge funds were being used for a personal purpose and that he could not retain the amount of the check.

In Brick v. Sovereign Grand Lodge, 196 Ark. 372, 117 S. W. 2d 1060 (1938), the Grand Master falsely represented that the Grand Lodge owed him some money and secured a note in the amount of the money claimed due; he then assigned the note to a third party. Suit was filed on the note. The court held the note to be invalid and held for the defendant.

In 1878 it appeared that there was a shortage in the account of the Grand Secretary of Illinois and he was indicted for the offense and in 1883 he was found guilty and sent to the state penitentiary. His sole defense was based on a technicality that the name of the Grand Lodge had omitted the word "ancient" in the title. The court held that this minor omission was not fatal to the suit.

It is customary for officers of an association who handle funds to give a surety bond. This has resulted in a number of cases filed to recover on these bonds. Here are a few illustrations of such cases.

In Torrent Lodge No. 711 v. National Surety Co., 231 Ky. 302, 21 S. W. 2d 439 (1929), suit was filed against a treasurer on a bond claiming a shortage in Lodge funds. Objection was made that the bond was given to the Grand Lodge, but that the suit had been filed by the new Lodge treasurer. The court held that the suit could be maintained in the name of the new treasurer. The wording of the bond was that it was given in favor of the Grand Lodge for the use of the Lodge.

In Sewell v. Brearhitt Lodge, 150 Ky. 542, 150 S. W. 677 (1912), suit was filed on a surety bond signed by a Lodge treasurer. He defended on the ground that at the time he signed the bond there was on it the signature of a co-surety, but that he had since found out that this signature was a forgery; that he relied on the genuineness of the other signature, and that he would not have signed the bond had he known of the forgery. The court held against him on this contention of the ground that the Lodge did not know of the forgery and it was not bound by any misrepresentation made on this behalf by one of its members.

In Western Indemnity Co. v. Free and Accepted Masons of Texas, 198 S. W. 1092 (1917, Tex. Viv. App.), a Grand Lodge of black men, calling themselves Masons, sued on a surety bond given by a Lodge treasurer. The company defended on the ground that the application for the bond, which had been signed by the Grand Master, contained false representations. After a consideration of all the evidence the court held in favor of the plaintiff on the ground that the Grand Lodge was not bound by the misrepresentation of the signer of the application.

In Bateman v. Sarbach, 89 Kans. 488, 132 Pac. 169 (1913), a Grand Treasurer signed a note and borrowed some money from a bank. He had no authority to sign the note or to borrow the money and he used the funds to cover up money which he had used for his personal purposes. Suit was filed on his bond. The jury, after hearing all the evidence, decided that the inaction of the Grand Lodge over a period of time amounted to a ratification of the transaction and the court found for the defendant.

In Masonic Mutual Benefit Society v. Strickland, 97 Mo. 137, 10 S. W. 895 (1899), suit was filed on a surety bond, and the court said on page 896, ". . . where the evidence is the result of voluminous facts, or of the inspection of many books and papers, the examination of which cannot conveniently take place in court, or where a witness has inspected the accounts of the parties, though not allowed to give evidence of the particular contents, he will be allowed to speak of the general balance or result of such examination, and such statement is not hearsay."

VI. MISCELLANEOUS CASES

One case of little legal significance but of great historical interest is King v. Parker, 9 Cush. (Mass.) 71 (1851), which involved the Green Dragon Tavern, meeting place of St. Andrew's Lodge, famous for many things, but especially noteworthy because this Lodge met on the evening of the Boston Tea Party and had to adjourn because a quorum was not present.

The Lodge in 1764 decided to buy the building. There were a number of conveyances for various reasons but eventually title was conveyed to five named persons, among them was Paul Revere, as Trustees, in joint tenancy. With the passage of time the grantees with Paul Revere being the last survivor and he died in 1818. Under the then existing law the title reverted to the heirs of William Burbeck, as so contended by his heirs many years later. In this case the court held that since the conveyance had been made to five grantees, as trustees, and the Lodge was the beneficiary of the trust, a court of equity would enforce the trust and give title to the Lodge.

In re MacKinley Lodge No. 840, 4 Fed Supp. 280 (1933), creditors of the Lodge filed a petition to have the Lodge declared a bankrupt. The court held that the Lodge was organized and was functioning in such a manner that it came within the provisions of the Bankruptcy Act and that the petition was properly filed.

There have been two cases in which suit was filed for damages claiming that the Masonic group had violated the patent of the plaintiff. In Masonic Fraternity Temple Association v. Murphy Iron Works, 215 Fed. 590 (1914), it was claimed that a self-feeding furnace used in an Illinois building violated the plaintiff's patent. In Masonic Hall and Asylum Fund v. Electrical Floor Box Corp., 218 Fed. 642 (1914), it was contended that the Trustees of a Masonic building violated a patent in connection with a floor box used to conduct electricity. Plaintiff won both cases.

In The Masonic Temple Association v. Farrar, 422 S. W. 2d 95 (1967, St. Louis Court of Appeals), a contract had been signed in 1917 by a number of Lodges and other groups of Masons to construct a Masonic Temple in St. Louis. A corporation was formed and the building was constructed. Because of changes in the area in 1959 one of the Lodges notified the Temple Association that it planned to move from the building. The Grand Master was requested to render help in solving the problem. He referred the matter to a committee of the Grand Lodge.

Extensive hearings were held with all interested parties taking part. The committee decided that it was not the type of dispute that the Grand Lodge ought to decide. The Temple Corporation then filed suit to secure the decision of the court. The court took the easy way out and decided that the various hearings had before the Grand Lodge Committee constituted submitting the controversy to arbitration at common law and that the decision of the committee was binding. Since the committee had decided on a "hands off" attitude, and the court indirectly adopted this decision, the effect was to decide in favor of the Lodge.

In People ex rel Bryant v. Zimmerman, 241 N. Y. 405 (1926), the court said on page 410, "But the Legislature may take notice of the potentialities of evil in secret societies, and may regulate them reasonably without depriving the members thereof of their liberty without due process of law . . . The Legislature must, however, adopt reasonable ground of classification in regulating such secret societies and organizations". This suit involved the Ku Klux Klan and the statute was held valid. The decision was affirmed in 279 U. S. 737 (1929).

There are two cases which have historical interest. In People v. Mather, 4 Wend. 229, 21 Am. Dec. 122 (1830, N. Y.), the defendant had been indicted in connection with the disappearance of William Morgan. Many technical matters relating to the qualifications of jurors to hear the case were considered in a long detailed opinion. The defendant was held not guilty. Unfortunately, the case does not summarize the facts presented at the trial.

In People v. Horton, 13 Wend. 9, 27 Am Dec. 167 (1834, N. Y.), a suit to recover damages for a claimed libel was filed and the question of the inability of a juror to serve was raised because of his Masonic membership since one of the parties was a former Mason. The interesting thing about the opinion is that it sets out in full the purported Masonic obligation.

In the Matter of John F. Tolle, Decisions of the Commissioner of Patents, 1872, page 219, the Commissioner refused to register as a trade mark certain words with a Masonic emblem in view of the magnitude of the Masonic organization and since it was not possible to separate associating this well known emblem with the Craft with its use as a trade mark. It was believed that its use would cause a deception.

In Ashley v. Board of Education, 275 Ill. 274 (1916), the court held that the children living in the Masonic Home could attend the local public school even though not domiciled at the Home. The controlling element was the actual place of residence of the child.

Miscellaneous Cases

In Leach v. Grinnell Savings Bank, 203 Iowa 235, 212 N. W. 485 (1927), the court held that a draft belonging to a Masonic Lodge and presented to an insolvent bank was not entitled to preference when a claim was filed.

In Roberta Lodge No. 204 v. Coleman, 188 Ark. 727, 67 S. W. 2d 578 (1934), the Lodge organized a committee to buy an old building to be remodeled for the use of the Lodge. Forty five dollars was collected from the members for this purpose. The matter was not completed because of lack of funds. But one of the committee members made arrangements to buy the property in his own name and he paid the full price. He informed the Lodge of what he had done. The Lodge took immediate steps to buy the property under the original terms and filed suit to have the deed to the committee member voided. The court held that good faith and fair dealing required the committee member not to profit from the arrangement behind the Lodge's back.

One non-Masonic case which is of interest because of possible analogy is La Rocca v. Lane, 77 Misc. 2d 123, 353 N. Y. S. 2d 867 (1974), in which a lawyer, who was also a clergyman, wore a clerical collar while trying a case. Objection was raised to his doing so. The court on appeal held it was not objectionable for the lawyer to do this.

As noted in the beginning, there are many more cases that could be considered. The manner in which the law is viewed changes almost daily, so there will be more cases involving fraternal organizations before this year is ended.

Here, however, we have a basis on which to work. We have cases that have stood the test of time.

APPENDIX

LIST OF CASES INVOLVING MASONIC BLACK GROUPS

Appeal of Woolford, 126 Pa. 47, 17 Atl. 524 (1889).
John A. Bell Grand Lodge v. M. W. St. John's Grand Lodge, 89 Okla. 112, 214 Pac. 114 (1923).
Bell v. Young, 20 S. W. 2d 135 (Tex. Civ. App., 1929).
Boozier v. McDonald, 177 S. W. 2d 807 (Tex. Civ. App., 1942).
Boozier v. McDonald, 177 S. W. 2d 809 (Tex. Civ. App., 1943).
Braden v. Lewis, 148 La. 920, 88 So. 117 (1921).
Braden v. Lewis, 149 La. 837, 90 So. 214 (1921).
Burrel v. Michaux, 273 S. W. 874 (Tex. Civ. App., 1925); 286 S. W. 176 (1926); 279 U. S. 737 (1929).
Cherry v. Bivens, 185 Miss. 329, 187 So. 525 (1939).
Cuney v. State, 142 Miss. 894, 108 So. 298 (1926).
Faisan v. Adair, 144 Ga. 797, 87 S. E. 1080 (1916); 148 Ga. 403, 96 S. E. 871 (871).
Free and Accepted Masons v. Ancient Free and Accepted Masons, 179 S. W. 265 (Tex. Civ. App., 1915).
Grand Lodge of Alabama v. Goodwin, 204 Ala. 213, 85 So. 553 (1920).
International Free and Accepted Modern Masons v. M. W. Prince Hall Grand Lodge, 318 S. W. 2d 46 (Ky. Ct. of App., 1958).
Knopp v. Sherwood, 239 App. Div. 475, 268 N. Y. S. 16 (1933).
Masonic Benefit Association of Stringer Grand Lodge v. Dotson, 111 Miss. 60, 71 So. 266 (1916).
Masonic Benefit Association of Stringer Grand Lodge v. First State Bank, 99 Miss. 610, 55 So. 408 (1911).
Minor v. St. John's Union Grand Lodge, 130 S. W. 893 (Tex. Civ. App. 1910).
M. W. Cuney Grand Lodge v. Knox, 144 Miss. 628, 109 So. 866 (1926).
M. W. Grand Lodge v. Callier, 224 Ala. 364, 140 So. 557 (1932).
M. W. Grand Lodge v. M. W. Prince Hall Grand Lodge, 90 W. Va. 424, 111 S. E. 309 (1922).
M. W. Hiram of Tyre Grand Lodge v. M. W. Sons of Light Grand Lodge, 94 Cal. App. 2d 25, 210 Pac. 2d 34 (1949).
M. W. Prince Hall Grand Lodge v. M. W. Universal Grand Lodge, 62 Wash. 2d 28 130 (1963).
M. W. King Solomon Grand Lodge v. M. W. Prince Hall Grand Lodge, 76 Colo. 469, 232 Pac. 664 (1925).

M. W. Prince Hall Grand Lodge v. M. W. Hiram Grand Lodge, 86 Colo. 17, 273 Pac 648 (1928).
M. W. Prince Hall Grand Lodge v. Supreme Grand Lodge, 105 F. Supp. 315, (1951), affd. 209 Fed 2d 156; cert. denied 347 U. S. 953.
M. W. United Grand Lodge v. Green, 136 Md. 582, 110 Atl. 851 (1920).
M. W. Grand Lodge v. West Temple Lodge, 43 Ariz. 57, 53 Pac. 2d 425 (1936).
M. W. Sons of Light Grand Lodge v. Sons of Light Lodge, 118 Cal. App. 2d 78, 257 Pac. 2d 464 (1953).
M. W. Hiram of Tyre Grand Lodge v. M. W. Sons of Light Grand Lodge, 94 Cal. App. 2d 25, 210 Pac. 2d 34 (1949).
M. W. United Grand Lodge v. Murphy, 139 Md. 225, 114 Atl. 876 (1921).
M. W. Widows Sons Grand Lodge v. M. W. Prince Hall Grand Lodge, 160 Pa. Super. 595, 52 Atl. 2d 333 (1947).
M. W. Grand Lodge v. Grimshaw, 34 App. D. of Col. 383 (1910).
Phillips v. Widows Son Lodge, 152 Va. 526, 147 S. E. 193 (1929).
Prince Hall Grand Lodge v. Supreme Council, 32 Misc. 2d 390, 227 N. Y. S. 841 (1962).
Prince Hall Grand Lodge v. M. W. King Solomon Grand Lodge, 62 N. M. 255, 308 Pac. 2d 581 (1957).
Prince Hall Grand Lodge v. M. W. Prince Hall Grand Lodge, 79 So. 2d 97 (La. Ct. of App., 1955).
St. Joseph's Grand Lodge v. M. W. St. John's Grand Lodge, 193 Okla. 283, 143 Pac. 2d 119 (1943).
The State v. Turner, 183 Kans. 469, 328 Pac. 2d 733 (1958).
State ex rel Hundley v. Goodwyn, 83 W. Va. 255, 98 S. W. 577 (1919).
Sunset Grand Lodge v. Bell, 25 S. W. 2d 160 (Tex. Civ. App., 1930).
Venus Lodge v. Acme Benevolent Assn., 231 N. C. 522, 58 S. E. 2d 109 (1950).
(These cases are analyzed and discussed in detail by H. W. Coil, Sr., a lawyer, in *A Documentary Account of Prince Hall and Other Black Fraternal Orders*, 1982).

BIBLIOGRAPHY

General Law Encyclopedias:
   Associations, 7 C. J. S. 19;
   Beneficial Association, 10 C. J. S. 249;
   Clubs, 14 C. J. S. 1279;
   Associations and Clubs, 6 Am. Juris. 2d 427;
   Fraternal Orders and Benevolent Societies, 36 Am. Juris. 2d 801;
   Freemason, 27 C. J. 897; 37 C. J. S. 1375;
   The American and English Encyclopedia of Law, 2d ed., Vol. 14, pp. 533-546 (1900).

Transactions of Quatuor Coronati Lodge:
   Fooks, William, "Freemasons in Reference to the Laws of the Realm,"
   5 A. Q. C. 88 (1892).
   Hextall, W. B., "The Craft in the Law Courts," 30 A. Q. C. 222 (1917).

Digests of The Masonic Service Association:
   "Spurious Freemasonry", 1st ed., 1934; 2nd ed., 1945.
   "Taxation of Masonic Property", 1st ed., 1932; 2nd ed., 1945.
   Cerza, Alphonse, "Freemasonry and Civil Law," 1953.
   ——, "Masonic Questions Answered by the Courts," 1972.
   "Incorporation of Grand Lodges and Lodges"

Miscellaneous Masonic Material:
   Evans, B. Evans, "The Thomson Masonic Fraud," 1922.
   Wiest, W. Irvine, *Freemasonry in the American Courts*, MLR, 1958
   Mackey's *Encyclopedia of Freemasonry*, Vol. 3, by H. L. Haywood, pp. 1283-1287.
   Hay, Arthur D., "Freemasonry in the Civil Courts," Transactions of the Research Lodge of Oregon.
   Cerza, Alphonse, "The Taxation of Masonic Property," Transactions of
   Walter F. Meier Lodge of Research, 1955.
   Coil, Sr., H. W., Sherman, John M. and Voorhis, Harold V. B.,*A
   Documentary Account of Prince Hall and Other Black Fraternal Orders,* (1982, Missouri Lodge of Research)
   Cerza, Alphonse, "What Penalty Can Be Imposed if a Non-Member Wears a Masonic Pin?" *Royal Arch Mason Magazine* (Spring, 1981)

——, "Women's Liberation" and Freemasonry, 1978, Research Lodge
No. 2
Lamb, Newell A., "Masonic Trials and Privileges Communications" "The Secret Societies Act of 1789," *Royal Arch Mason*, (1954)

American Law Reports Annotated:
"Exemption from Taxation of Property of Fraternal or Religious Association", 22 ALR 907 (1923); 38 ALR 36 (1925); 83 ALR 768 (1933)
"Compelling Admission of Membership in Professional Association or
Society", 89 ALR 2d 964
"Contributions, Personal Liability on, of Member of Voluntary Association not Organized for Personal Profit", 41 ALR 754 (1926)
"Effect of Injunction Restraining Expulsion", 1 ALR 169 (1919)
"Expulsion from Professional Association", 20 ALR 2d 531 (1951)
"Expulsion from Social Club or Similar Society", 20 ALR 2d 344 (1951)
"Expulsion or Suspension of Local Lodge or Other Unit of Benefit Society", 94 ALR 639 (1935)
"Liability of Members for Distribution of Property of Defunct Association or Club Contrary to Rules therefore", 168 ALR 962 (1947)
"Meaning of Phrase 'In Good Standing' employed in Contract of Mutual Benefit Association with Member", 23 ALR 340 (1923)
"Notice of Hearing Before Suspension or Expulsion. Right of
Member of Society With Benefits in Nature of Insurance", 27 ALR 1512 (1923)
"Notice of Hearing as Affecting Expulsion from Social Club or Similar Society", 20 ALR 2d 353 (1951)
"Power and Capacity of Members of Unincorporated Association, Lodge, Society, or Club to Convey, Transfer, or Encumber Association Property", 15 ALR 2d 1451 (1951)
"Recovery by Member from Unincorporated Association for Injuries Inflicted by Tort of Fellow Member", 14 ALR 2d 473 (1950)
"Remedies for Determining Right or Title to Office in Unincorporated Private Association", 82 ALR 2d 1169 (1962)
"Resignation of Membership in Club or Other Non-Profit Association", 99 ALR 1444 (1935)
"Right to Assets of Defunct or Voluntary Dissolved Club", 68 ALR 956 (1947)

Bibliography

"Right to Damages for Exclusion from Membership in Social Organization", 59 ALR 2d 1920 (1958)

"Rights and Liabilities Arising out of Contract for Lifetime Membership in Social or Fraternal Club or Association", 10 ALR 3rd 1357 (1966)

"Right to Discipline Member for Exercising A Right or Performance of Duty as a Citizen", 14 ALR 1446 (1921)

"Second Trial by Association for Same Offense", 1 ALR 431 (1919)

"Suitability of Individual Members of Unincorporated Association as Affected by Statute or Rule permitting Association to Be Sued as an Entity", 92 ALR 499 (1963)

"Suspension or Expulsion from Social Club or Similar Society and Remedies Therefore", 20 ALR 2d 344 (1951)

"Suspension or Expulsion from Church or Religious Society and the Remedies Therefore", 20 ALR 2d 421 (1951)

"Rights and Remedies in Respect of Membership in American Legion or Other Veteran Organization", 147 ALR 590 (1943)

"Tax Exemption of Property Used by Fraternal or Benevolent Association for Clubhouse or Similar Purpose", 39 ALR 3rd 640 (1971)

"Tax on Dues or Membership Fees; What is a Social Club Within Statute Imposing?" 80 ALR 1296 (1932); 135 ALR 1173 (1941)